Tamar leads the way !

Healing Hurting Women

Dorothy M. Guy

1

First published in the United Kingdom

This edition published by Tamar Ministry Healing
Hurting Women 2006

Dorothy Guy asserts the moral right to be identified
as the author of this book

ISBN 0-9552397-0-2
078-0-9552397-0-0

© Copyright Dorothy M Guy

A catalogue record for this book is available from the
British Library

Printed and bound in Great Britain
by Irongate Digital Solutions

Illustrations by Danielle Blake

Scripture quotations are from the New International
Version of the Bible (NIV)

ACKNOWLEDGEMENTS

From the outset I would like to thank Almighty God for His unfailing loving-kindness, mercy and blessings upon my life.

I am appreciative for the un-abating inspiration that the Sovereign Lord and His Holy Spirit has given me to write the book.

I would like to thank my two special angels, Danielle and Othnielle. Without their great contributions, hard work, support, love and prayers the success would not have been as great.

I thank Bishop Donald Bernard, Bishop Danny Bennett, Marion Best, Pastor Yvonne Frith, my many friends and fellow workers especially of the Tamar Ministry, and not forgetting Pauline Byers, Leonie Moukodi and Cynthia Henry for their willing and resourceful support so readily given.

May the electrifying feelings that sparked me to write, propel you to read and help you to make the transition.

3

CONTENTS

ABOUT THE AUTHOR

Undeterred by her own heart breaking experiences, Dorothy is the epitome of a woman who is not prepared to remain where non-good wishers want her to be.

She exhibits all the necessary characteristics of someone who fights back and wins, trusting solely in the Most High God.

She has been going to extraordinary lengths to assist women who are hurting and in need of healing.

She draws inspiration from the word of God in the Bible, nature and others around her.

Dorothy encourages everyone to believe that nothing is set in stone and that believing in their own dreams and a lot of effort will undoubtedly transport them to the top. She offers invaluable words of encouragement and wisdom on how to trust in the infallible word of God to guaranteed success.

HOW TO USE THIS BOOK

This book should be your constant companion on the journey to victory and supremacy.

Read, meditate, fast and pray to witness lasting change. Memorise the scripture verses. Make your personal notes if you have to, as to what the passage is saying to you!

Each chapter should be a lesson to your personal growth, development and enlightenment.

Keep a record of your progress in order to offer yourself comfort, when healing seems detached and is out of your grasp.
You are not a waste of space or a loser.
You were born to win!

PREFACE

Praise be to the Lord God, the God of Israel, who
alone does marvellous deeds. Psalm 72:18 (NIV)
Finding a lit path after groping in the dark is
reassuring, as it gives hope for much anticipated
progress.
Finding fruitful trees with ripened edible fruit is
comforting to the stomach, especially when faced
with dire hunger and thirst.
Finding the gift of life growing inside the womb
is magical, as barrenness limits the genealogy of
the future.
Finding oneself entangled in the twist and turns
of life can be mind-boggling. Sadness and trials
have a way of hand picking their victims without
prior warning or appointment. It can be
devastating, leaving many feeling out of their
depth to effectively fight back victoriously.
This publication comes at a time when the cry of
many hurting women, who are in pain, and
looking for answers to their own problems are
able to look in the pages of this book, and it is my

prayer that they can examine the life- path of especially the woman Tamar. Who wins against all odds and by the Divine help of God make the necessary personal adjustments to also be a winner.

INTRODUCTION

The woman Tamar and her life journey as documented in the Bible, read in my spirit like a thriller. It is, in my opinion, filled with great expectations. Her dreams come true, to be the chosen bride of the renowned family of the land Judah.

Tamar roller-coasted into repeated set backs and sadness. She is banished from her new family and community and given false hope at the hand of the respected leader of the day, who is also her father-in-law. She looks hopelessly through the window, listening attentively for her name to be called; but to no avail.

Ultimately Tamar takes the risk to move her life on the best way she is able to, without guidance, support or encouragement.

She faced, possibly, the worse days of her life, as she took her place with the lower classes of society's 'prostitutes'. She skilfully secured her future in the process by becoming pregnant. She escaped death by fire, broke forth at child birth, later clinching the inheritance due to her children, setting the stage for renowned kings to come forth and, more importantly, rose to the hall of fame in the genealogy of Jesus Christ.

This fortune is not just for the lucky few but for those who have the guts and courage to push against the barriers set up to hinder their progress. Jabez, in 1 Chronicles: 4:10 NIV inspired us to reach out and accept our blessings at the hand of God's mercy and loving-kindness. "Oh, that you would bless me and enlarge my territory! Let your hand be with me, and keep me from harm so that I will be free from pain." And God granted his request.

The struggle of life is one that most, if not all human beings will some day experience, some more vividly, others covertly, but none can boast that they have been exempt from daily sorrows. How we deal with challenges, difficulties and pains is a matter of choice. One person may rely on instinct, family and friends, another on mysticism, philosophy and other forms of art.

I, for the purpose of this book, rely on the word of God as listed in the Bible and on the Holy Spirit of God to propel me into the unknown of blessings stored up for me and for you, who will invite the Lordship of Christ to aid you through your many heartaches and heavy burdens.

Today sets the stage for a brighter tomorrow. Our Abba Father in Heaven is responsible to help us, His children, who ask it of Him.

The Genesis story of Tamar and Judah is the under girding to this book. Support will be pulled from scriptures and life's general experiences.

CHAPTER 1

<u>FAMILY CIRCLE</u>

The actual nature of the family unit is as ordained by God for the comfort and protection of its members. The group is usually made up of blood relatives but in Christendom; the members of the body of Christ are also viewed as family.

EXAMINE FOR YOURSELF whether these rules are still relevant today and if so which are you adhering to with your family? Exodus: 20: 1-17 (The Ten Commandments)

1 And God spoke all these words: *2* "I am the LORD your God, who brought you out of Egypt, out of the land of slavery. *3* "You shall have no other gods before me.

4 "You shall not make for yourself an idol in the form of anything in heaven above or on the earth beneath or in the waters below. 5 You shall not bow down to them or worship them; for I, the LORD your God, am a jealous God, punishing the children for the sin of the fathers to the third and fourth generation of those who hate me, 6 but showing love to a thousand {generations} of those who love me and keep my commandments.

7 "You shall not misuse the name of the LORD your God, for the LORD will not hold anyone guiltless who misuses his name.

8 "Remember the Sabbath day by keeping it holy. 9 Six days you shall labor and do all your work, 10 but the seventh day is a Sabbath to the LORD your God. On it you shall not do any work, neither you, nor your son or daughter, nor your manservant or maidservant, nor your animals, nor the alien within your gates. 11 For in six days the LORD made the heavens and the earth, the sea, and all that is in them, but he rested on the seventh day. Therefore the LORD blessed the Sabbath day and made it holy.

12 "Honor your father and your mother, so that you may live long in the land the LORD your God is giving you. 13 "You shall not murder. 14 "You shall not commit adultery. 15 "You shall not steal. 16 "You shall not give false testimony against your neighbor. 17 "You shall not covet your neighbor's house. You shall not covet your neighbor's wife, or his manservant or maidservant, his ox or donkey, or anything that belongs to your neighbor."

FAMILY CIRCLE

The Divine plan of God for the family has been, from the beginning of time, to keep us together, well nurtured and cared for, protected, loved and to learn and pass on values from one generation to the next. All Nations, People and leaders have modelled this idea in one form or another, as this has proven to work and has been an important part of society's foundations, stability, growth and continuity.

> "God sets the lonely in families, He leads forth the prisoners with singing; but the rebellious live in a sun-scorched land."
> Psalm 68:6 NIV

Here we see the wisdom of God displayed for all to see, as He gathered the lonely and placed them where they can feel a sense of belonging and a part of a circle of like-minded people. The prisoners have a bright future also as they are led with singing, but the rebellious will have a hard time, due to failure to comply with God's family life plan. Look at the list below and tick the kind of family you are in and analyse its future for you:

POSITIVE	NEGATIVE
Place of protection	Place of threats
Security	Abuse
Laughter	Sadness
Making merry	Making crime
Nurturing	Being stunted
Success	Failure
Bestowal	Deprivation
Love	Violence and Hatred
Peace	War

Over significant decades, the female has suffered more in the family than their male counterpart. Being perceived as the weaker vessel they have been subjected to despicable ill treatment, which has led to multiple hurts and pains.
The bottom line of hurt is that it robs individuals of reaching their God given potential, to be all that God has intended for them to be and excel to their highest.

The cycle of hurt and pains can and must be broken. The power is within you to rise from the situation, a much stronger, determined and rounded person.
Use your personal life experience to move yourself on. You are indeed a survivor, with great potential and God has given you the power to assist others with confidence, but only if you recognise that you do not have to do it all by yourself.

The Lord is with you to help you and more importantly, you are now an adult and not the helpless, dependent and vulnerable young person that you once were. Therefore do not give anyone the authority to continue to take advantage of you, even if you are somewhat likely to be dependent on others. Pray to God always to escape their trap; you are precious and a priceless individual.

The word of God said: "In the same way, the Spirit helps us in our weakness. We do not know what we ought to pray for, but the Spirit Himself intercedes for us with groans that words cannot express. And he who searches our hearts knows the mind of the Spirit, because the Spirit intercedes for the saints in accordance with God's will."
Romans 8:26-27 NIV.

VALUE ME

The changing face of family life, society's demands with regard to socio-economic advancement, housing, migration and many other factors, has placed the onus on us as women to be the main pillar of the family circle; the home maker, care giver, educator and so on and further more, to embrace and celebrate the great value that is embedded within us, initially to help heal our own pains and hurts and to assist those around us less able to do so for the good of all.

The life of many women who are hurting can be imagined as, being on the highway, we either get on it and make the necessary progress or dither and stay off it and are left behind. The life of Tamar with Judah sets the scene for us as individual family and friends, to walk according to the doors Jesus set open for us to be healed from our every condition, or to negate the opportunity given to us to fulfil our purpose and destiny.

There are many great values locked within a woman, made in the image of God. Women are therefore encouraged to embrace the validation of God which states: "Then the Lord God made a woman from the rib He had taken out of the man, and He brought her to the man." Genesis: 2:22 NIV. Women! Only God knows of your beginning and of your end.

The Sovereign Lord is the only one who has full knowledge of our Deoxyribonucleic Acid (DNA); He is our Maker and the one who has the ultimate responsibility for our life existence.

Cry if you must, bawl if you must, wail if you must, scream if you must, shout if you must, in fact do whatever you must but when you are through, you must rise up and you must take control for your advancement!

Background

It is essential that the establishment of any family members be made clear so as to avoid confusion. Judah is the fourth son of Jacob and Leah. His mother Leah was not loved either by her father Laban or by Jacob her husband. Judah's name means 'praise'; he is from a family of twelve siblings. Judah left the family unit shortly after his brother Joseph was sold into slavery.

Judah joined himself with a man of Adullam by the name of Hirah. Judah later met with a wealthy Canaanite man named Shuah and so he married Shuah's daughter.

Judah and Shuah's marriage produced three sons namely:

Er meaning watchful

Onan meaning strong

and Shelah, the youngest of the siblings and still a child, meaning petition.

Here we see a new family being formed and extending with great hopes and prospects. As the young men mature, the need to fulfil the creation plan takes precedence and so Judah sought a wife for his oldest son Er, as was the custom.

THE CHOICE BRIDE

Tamar was identified as the choice and chaste bride for Er. Her name means palm tree or cluster.

The preparation for the wedding is traditionally one of the most exciting time in a young woman's life.

Betrothal was the first stage of public announcement of the intention of the couple to get married. Choosing the right woman was not left to chance or done in an ad hoc way. The background of the family would have been fully explored and so would the couple's personal standing. For Judah, selecting the right partner for his son was crucial and paramount, as he needed to preserve the clan to which he belonged; so that the blessings of Yahweh would follow him in the new country he had settled down in to extend the family circle.

The dream to be with the man of her desire, to look the perfect part, to walk with the chosen bridal party, even if it was arranged, had an edge of real importance and excitement for Tamar.

Judah and his wife Shuah must have felt very proud of the choice they had made for their first-born son Er. Judah was fully aware of his value.

So, in keeping with the promise of God for his family linage, as a called out and chosen people, Judah was aware that staying in the Will of God was compulsory for the preservation of a righteous race. Hence, he chose a bride who had pedigree qualities and who would no doubt add to the family renowned and ultimately to fulfilling God's purpose for the patriarchs, as given to Abraham.

With marriage comes gift of various degrees and according to the Jewish custom of the day, the chance for the new wife to join her husband's family and leave hers behind; a heart wrenching time for the bride but one that is a must.

GREAT EXPECTATION

Tamar, in my view, went into the marriage and this family with high hopes. She knew that after marriage everyone would be keeping an eye on her as to whether she was pregnant or not. After the bliss the subtle pressure of others wanting to know if you are pregnant or not gets in the way. In the close proximity and under the watchful eye of a new family, I can just imagine the weight this must have been for Tamar.

She has no immediate power to change the under currents of situations at play and, like us, feels powerless to alter what exactly is going on. This is because Er is getting up to things that the naked eyes of his parents, siblings, wider family
members and community are unaware of.

Tamar may be feeling troubled, worried and out of her depth as to whether to do or say anything concerning the secrets of the bedroom.
There is a scary notion that things are not going

too well in the bedroom. Judah especially, was aware of the royal seed that is to come from his family, and so Judah thought that Er was the person earmarked as the carrier of the royal seed.

Often as human beings we get things wrong, as our finite knowledge is limited. Therefore, it is imperative that we rely heavily on the infinite wisdom and guidance of God, to navigate the path before us so we do not prejudice and sentence others wrongly, according to our own feelings, rules and regulations.

The word of the Lord reminds us: "Do not judge, or you too will be judged. For in the same way as you judge others, you will be judged, and with the measure you use, it will be measured to you." Matthew 7:1-2 NIV

No family unit is exempt from the usual sorrows of life, but the way that we make each other feel is a matter of choice. The power is invested in us to enhance each other lives, without singling out our favourites for the better treatment and dishing out the worse of our disdain to the unloved ones.

All God's chosen women have the potential to bring forth royal seeds, when placed in the right environment, with the right partner and with the fertile favour of God's approval. Could anything possibly go wrong when the path for Tamar and Er seems so promising? They look glowing, definitely in love, full of the joys of life like the sun glistening on ripened fruits.

It is imperative that all of God's women recognise that each was born to fulfil a purpose that no one else can do. It has been invested in us to overcome life's obstacles, testing and trials.

I stress to you, who are hurting and are within a family, be it biological, adopted or by choice of fellowship, to look beyond the buzzing sounds of distasteful memories that seem to want to destroy you.

Find your rightful place, purpose and usefulness in the fellowship of Christ Himself and the family He has hewed out for your love, general care and welfare and also your peace of mind.

Do stop the pondering, worrying and getting yourself frustrated and begin to acknowledge the power and skills invested in you because God has made you precious and valuable.

Therefore, dry up your tears and use your energy to put strategies in place that will change you and your future well-being in this evolving world.

You know what they say; 'a change is as good as a rest'.

The supreme wisdom of God in many situations is in very short supply. To effectively affect change and make sound judgments in problematic cases in our era is a challenge.

King Solomon was one of the most prominent human beings that God had ever endowed with the wisdom of supremacy. This was clearly demonstrated in the cases of the two prostitutes who gave birth in close proximity. One of them killed her child by rolling onto, the child, as the babies were in the same beds as their mothers.

When the mother of the dead baby realised what had happened, she switched her dead baby with the other lady's live child.

This matter became a battle ground as dishonesty took centre stage, so much so that King Solomon was consulted to judge the matter.

The mother whose child was dead had a wicked spirit and refused to abate her strong argument that would have assisted in the right decision being reached earlier.

Solomon skilfully applied a method that was very unconventional. He called for a sword to split the live child and share among the women. The woman whose child was dead invited the act to take place, whilst the real mother could not accommodate this madness. Here is the account:

"The woman whose son was alive was filled with compassion for her son and said to the King, 'please, my lord, give her the living baby! Don't kill him!' But the other said, 'Neither I nor you shall have him. Cut him in two!'

Then the King gave his ruling: 'Give the living baby to the first woman. Do not kill him; she is his mother."

1 Kings 3:26-27 NIV

From my personal experience, I believe the wicked woman was a smooth talker. She behaved convincingly and perhaps had a pitiful persuasive facial expression. Equally, she may have behaved calmly, calculating but deadly.

In circumstances of this nature I can advise you to invoke the Sovereign Lord to vindicate your case. To try and convince the converted against their misleading conclusion, can be just as perplexing as the wicked woman's act.

CHAPTER 2

<u>SHADOW OF DEATH</u>

"Bitterly she weeps at night, tears are upon her cheeks. Among all her lovers there is none to comfort her. All her friends have betrayed her; they have become her enemies."

Lamentations 1:2 NIV

REALITY POINT: Shadow that is not your own engenders panic, fear, worry and suspicion.

EVIDENCE: *"Even though I walk through the valley of the shadow of death, I will fear no evil, for you are with me; your rod and your staff, they comfort me"*.

EXPLANATION: Whenever we are faced with the unknown our natural instinct takes over and causes us to feel and think weird. The truth of the matter is if you plant sound words like in this Psalm in your heart and repeat them loudly in times of trouble, you will find instant comfort and reassurance. Look carefully at the personal claims made in the Psalm of <u>My</u>, <u>I</u> and <u>Me</u>   Psalm 23:1-6

1 The LORD is my shepherd, I shall not be in want. *2* He makes me lie down in green pastures, he leads me beside quiet waters, *3* he restores my soul.   He guides me in paths of righteousness for his name's sake.   *4* Even though I walk through the valley of the shadow of death,   I will fear no evil, for you are with me; your rod and your staff,   they comfort me.   *5* You prepare a table before me in the presence of my enemies. You anoint my head with oil; my cup overflows.   *6* Surely goodness and love will follow me
all the days of my life, and I will dwell in the house of the LORD forever.

Death speaks of finality, it is therefore imperative that we recognize the steps to take when the shadows are hanging around in order to make amends so that we escape death grips.

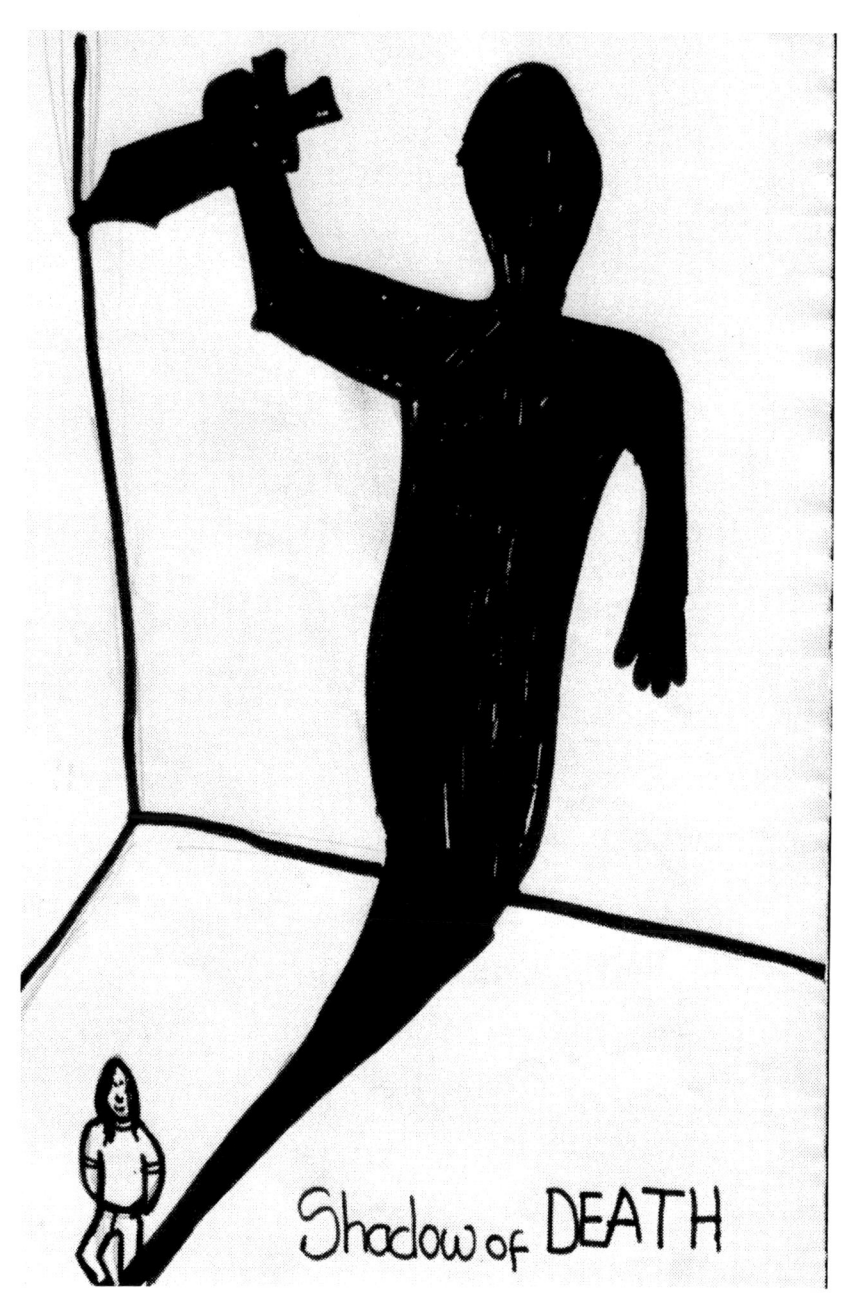

Shadow of DEATH

SHADOW OF DEATH

With a dramatic descent of a sudden change in the atmosphere, like that of dusk unexpectedly appearing, so the dense darkness and chillness of death fell upon Tamar's husband Er.

The word of the Lord comes to straighten us up, and point the way to the Divine order of God. It states: " His eyes are on the ways of men; He sees their every step. There is no dark place, no deep shadow, where evildoers can hide."

Job 34: 21-22 NIV

The enemies of death surrounded Tamar and Judah's household with little or no chance of them escaping its attack, as Er had left himself open to be infiltrated with Satan's incitements to displease God and His order. Consequently, Er plunged himself into deliberately violating and sinning against the Most High God.

Life and nature have a way of rapidly changing their cosmic motion and leaving us humans with more questions than answers.

The brain has not the capacity to fully prepare itself for the unthinkable, heart wrenching pains that disappointment, failure and death does from time to time throw up.

Having then the insight of this revelation and understanding, God wants us to keep in mind that: "The eyes of the Lord are everywhere, keeping watch on the wicked and the good"

Proverbs 15:3 NIV

SHOCKING DEATH OF ER

There is no sign of sickness with Er, in fact he presented
perfectly well and healthy only a moment before.
But Er is now dead and it was very sudden.

The cause of death is inconclusive according to the medical
pathologist's findings.

Unknown to man, "… Er, Judah's firstborn, was wicked in
the Lord's sight; so the Lord put him to death."
Genesis 38:7 NIV

Back on planet earth, the thick black curtain of sadness,
weeping and mourning is heard all around.
What happened? What happened? I imagine, was the
unanswered question of the day.

Tamar is left dumb struck as to what to tell Er's parents, the
immediate and extended family members, friends and the
wider community. All are anxiously waiting to hear some
coherent news that makes sense.

Did Er die naked or clothed? But what has this to
do with his death? Just surmising as to what else may be at
play at the time of his last hour with his wife Tamar.

In Tamar's defence, she does not recall Er being off colour
or complaining of feeling unwell. Everyone is baffled and
shocked at the headline news of Er's death.
Through the gloom, the burial took place. Gradually the
shocking news is wearing off about Er's swift departure.
The curious gazing eyes, look on to see if there is any sign
of Tamar developing a stomach; but to no avail.

Tamar's brief moment with her husband was short lived.
She is now alone, bewildered, widowed and childless,
perhaps walking around dolefully and looking dejected.

It is speculated that Judah enters into further dialogue with
his wife Shua in order to decide the future fate of Tamar
among them, seeing that her reason for being with them has
now changed, as her husband is dead and has not any
offspring after him.

LEVIRATE MARRIAGE

Levirate marriage was legitimate

in the custom that this family lived in.

The definition is as outlined below.

'Levirate marriage is the practice of a woman marrying

one of her husband's sons or brothers after her

husband's death, in order to continue his line. Levirate

marriage has been practiced by societies with a strong

clan structure in which exogamous marriage outside

the clan was forbidden. Groups that have practiced

levirate marriage include the Israelites.'

Ruth and Boaz are examples of Levirate marriage.

Judah, having reached a decision with what to do with

Tamar and her future well-being within his family,

instructed Onan to: "Lie with your brother's wife and fulfil

your duty to her as a brother in-law to produce offspring for

your brother.'

Genesis 38:8 NIV

The children born within a Levirate relationship belong to the deceased brother, thus the share of the inheritance due to the heir would go to the children and the levirate husband would have no inheritance.

THE LIFE AND DEATH OF ONAN

Judah, being versed in the Levirate custom, gave impetus to
Onan his second son and brother of Er to be Tamar's second
husband.

Once again the sound of joy, singing, laughter, general
happiness returned to the household where Tamar was
residing. The expected great dream and aspiration that
Tamar would be bringing forth the royal seed had been
resurrected in the minds of the hopeful.

The marriage has by now taken place. Tamar and Onan
seem to be the next best perfect couple to be imitated. At
least for this moment it seems that the valley experience that
Tamar feels she was plunged into, when the tentacles of
death engulfed her and her dreams with her first husband's,
has temporarily faded.

Judah told Onan to: "Lie with your brother's wife and fulfil
your duty to her as a brother-in-law to produce offspring for
your brother." Genesis 38:8 NIV

I see here that the months are swiftly passing by. The couple seem relatively happy together but there is still no sign of the real reason for them being together. Tamar is not showing signs of being a fruitful woman. I believe it is worth noting here that the subtle pressure is mainly imposed on the woman and that in our biased societies, lack of fruitfulness is scarcely seen as the man's fault.

God is nonetheless helping us to make amends. "He said: Take heed, you senseless ones among the people; you fools, when you become wise? Does He who implanted the ear not hear? Does He who forms the eye not see..."
Psalm 94:8-9 NIV

Tamar, it seems, may be feeling too embarrassed to tell anyone outside the bedroom what exactly is going on. Often women remain silent thus endorsing the status quo, of being discreet, sweet and all that others conjure up an image for her to be. Apart from all this she is not having a good name among the general public, due to the silent muttering that is possibly taking place, as it does in a clannish community.

The initial shroud of darkness has returned and is hanging over as it did before. I believe that Tamar was having the premonition that her marriage to Onan was also on unsteady foundation. Furthermore, it seems that these brothers' bedroom habits were bringing concerns and silent pains to the moral, spiritual and physical expectations of Tamar's limited intimate exposure to men.

Onan's own selfishness and refusal to comply with married life's expectation for procreation plunged him into disaster with his maker, the Lord of Host. "But Onan knew that the offspring would not be his; so whenever he lay with his brother's wife, he spilled his semen on the ground to keep from producing offspring for his brother. What he did was wicked in the Lord's sight; so He put him to death also." Genesis 38:9-10 NIV

Judah, oblivious to his second son's behaviour and practice, as was the case before, in the midst of his grief, wasted no time in making a firm decision to send Tamar packing to her own father's care.

Just when Tamar perhaps felt that life could not get any worse, she is now coping with a double whammy of sorrows that she has no explanation for.

The straggling jolts of heartache, sorrow and pain are determined to plunge Tamar deeper and deeper into the abyss, beyond her personal life preparation and experience. This kind of trauma can be a disabling blow for the world's strongest and determined person.

It is at this desperate hour that the only true solace is to be found in the Divine intervention of God's infallible word:

"The heavens praise your wonders, O Lord, your faithfulness too, in the assembly of the holy ones. For who in the skies above can compare with the Lord? Who is like the Lord among the heavenly beings? In the council of the holy ones God is greatly feared; He is more awesome than all who surround Him. O Lord God Almighty, who is like you? You are mighty, O Lord, and your faithfulness surrounds you." Psalm 89:5-8 NIV

DOUBLE BEREAVEMENTS

In my reflection on what seemed to be the catastrophic events of Tamar's private and public life, I believe that no prior knowledge or wisdom could have prepared her for what was and is to come.

The loss of any member of a family pains the heart, more so of one that has joined flesh with your flesh. This is a double blow, as no one else can come as close to bind up Tamar's broken heart. This then is the job of the Lord Himself who affirmed that: "The Spirit of the Sovereign Lord is on me, because the Lord has anointed me to preach good news to the poor. He has sent me to bind up the broken-hearted, to proclaim freedom for the captives and release from darkness for the prisoners, to proclaim the year of the Lord's favour and the day of vengeance of our God, to comfort all who mourn, and provide for those who grieve in Zion- to bestow on them a crown of beauty instead of ashes, the oil of gladness instead of mourning and a garment of praise instead of a spirit of despair. They will be called oaks of righteousness, a planting of the Lord for the display of His splendour."

Isaiah 61:1-3 NIV

Bereavement is not just about physical death but also multiple losses. Tamar was undoubtedly definitely suffering from many losses; loss of inheritance, loss of the opportunity to bear a child as was expected, loss of status within the community, lost prominence with family members and the wider community, loss of loved ones and friends who may have trusted her and are now doubting the lack of explanation that has been made available to all.

Judah equally suffered, as later his wife Shua died and he was put in a grief stricken position also. So let us be mindful that today is for me and tomorrow may be yours, or vice versa.

Just let us reflect for a while; for if Tamar was someone who was prone to depression, stress, anxiety, panic attacks, phobia and the like, she would be a nervous wreck. These pressures are real and can be compounded when you are with a group that is casting a weight of doubt on your credibility and genuineness.

GOSSIP

The swirling cords of gossip, the bitter words of accusations and the malicious muttering of busy bodies can all too often oppress the uninvited victim, almost to the edge of despair and hopelessness.

The word of Solomon said: "The words of a gossip are like choice morsel; they go down to a man's inmost parts." Proverbs18:8 NIV.

Developing resilience against gossip is challenging and frustrating to the soul. Gossip is influential, hence it often chokes and stifles those who are caught up in it and who have been isolated to be freely talked about.

Gossip has the power to produce a fertile ground for hatred and scorn, for the person that has been targeted to be gossiped about, be it covert or overt. Gossip does not leave room for love, protection and or kindness. It has no mercy, no compassion and no grace. Sadly, such qualities are often rife in Christian and religious settings, as in the world at large.

Consequently, the Lord Himself is the only one who has the supremacy to turn the wicked nature of gossip from the mouth of His people and give them lasting redemption that states:

"Fear not, for I have redeemed you; I have summoned you by name, you are mine. When you pass through the waters I will be with you; and when you pass through the rivers, they will not sweep over you. When you walk through the fire, you will not be burned; the flames will not set you ablaze.

For I am the Lord your God…" Isaiah 43:..1-3.. NIV.

Therefore, rest assured that God is in control of greater issues than gossip, so you will and must overcome those who take delight in talking about you wrongfully!

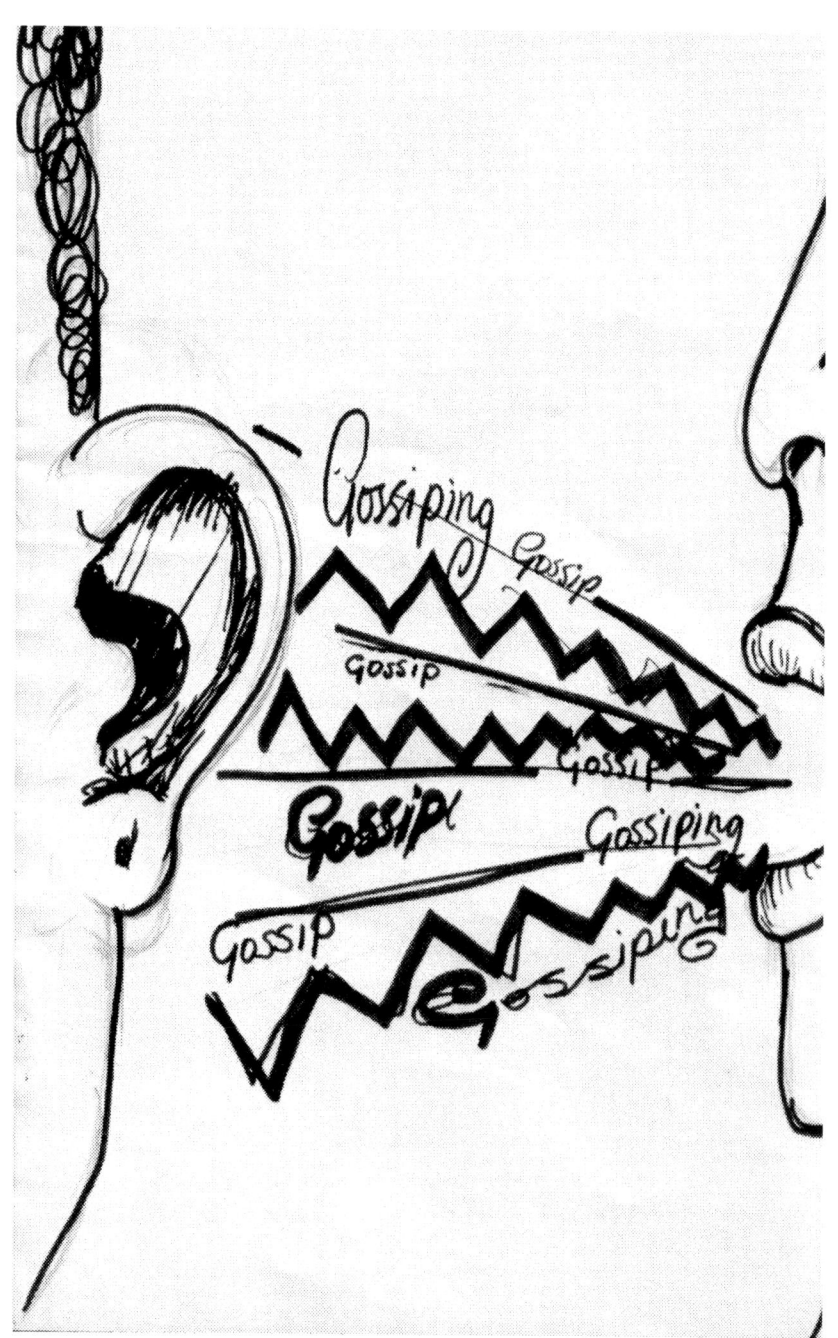

CHAPTER 3

<u>TRICKERY AND BANISHMENT</u>

There is no wisdom, no insight, no plan that can succeed against the Lord.

Proverbs 21:30 NIV

Trickery and Banishment

TRICKERY AND BANISHMENT

The initial hurdle that humanity had to deal with was the great trickery of Satan, in the garden of Eden. Many unwise comments have been made as to Adam and Eve's role in succumbing to the incitement of Satan, to sin against God's command by eating of the forbidden fruit in the garden.

The blame culture is one that is as old as at the beginning of creation. "Now the serpent was crafty than any of the wild animals the Lord God had made." He said to the woman, "Did God really say, 'you must not eat from any tree in the garden'?" Genesis 3:1 NIV

Trickery is an ingenious device to cunningly divert the other person's attention in order to gain control of them or their possessions.

Satan is the father of illusionary tricks; he mischievously secured the removal of both Adam and Eve from their paradise home. In like manner he is seeking to secure his position to remove you from your birthright ordained by God for His glory in you and through you.

Tamar is given no choice but to comply with Judah's request for her to leave the family circle. " Judah then said to his daughter-in-law Tamar, "Live a widow in your father's house until my son Shelah grows up." For he thought, "He may die too, just like his brothers." So Tamar went to live in her father's house."

Genesis 38:11 NIV.

No human being was a witness to the secrets of Judah's heart. With his voice he conveyed hope, perhaps in his communication he conveyed concern but in his mind he concluded with a deadly thought, that never in a million years would Tamar be coming back to be a part of his immediate family unit.

Judah's father Jacob had tricked his own father Isaac to secure the birthright. Laban, Jacob's father-in-law, tricked him by giving him Leah, instead of his choice love, Rachel. Now we see Judah suffering from the same fate as that of his father. With the trickery comes the banishment, as they are items that cannot be separated, they work best hand in hand.

Judah appeared to have in his genetic make-up the blueprint, skills and ability to trick Tamar 'good and proper'. He got Tamar to leave his home with the false promise that it would only be temporary, until Shelah was old enough to assume the Levirate way of Marriage.

It is my experience that men, in particular have surplus abilities to use tricks to their advantage and almost every time to divert the woman's attention from focussing on them and on their behaviour.

Their charm, charisma, wooing nature etc, has left many women wounded beyond repair. Tamar perhaps adopted the motto 'if I can't beat him, I will join him.' I would say to those of you who are feeling cornered and confused, look for the next opportunity to make your advantageous and progressive move out of that situation. Never, and I repeat, never accept what life throws at you and do nothing about it; rise up like the following men did.

"Now there were four men with leprosy at the entrance of the city gate. They said to each other, "Why stay here until we die?" 2 kings 7:3 NIV

If the sick leprous men were able to actively make plans to move their lives on, should not also the daughters of Abraham be doing the same? Today is the day to make a firm positive decision. Get up woman and do it, you can, successfully, with God's help!

LEAVING THE FAMILIAR

It is not easy to leave people whom you have spent many years with, without feeling sad, uncertain and fearful. It is even worse when the circumstances are not good, when you are aware that returning is not an option, as you would not be made to feel welcome as was the case before the breakdown occurred.

Ruth 1:16-17 NIV, Points the way to a lasting and bonding relationship with her mother-in-law Naomi. "Don't urge me to leave you or to turn back from you. Where you go I will go, and where you stay I will stay. Your people will be my people and your God my God. Where you die I will die, and there I will be buried. May the Lord deal with me, be it ever so severely, if anything but death separates you and me."

What a beautiful covenant of commitment. This is certainly not an every day occurrence. Being ostracised is more the norm especially in strong, dominant, religious circles, where, if any one fails to comply with the consensus of the masses, their lives would be made difficult by the pressures imposed to bring isolation, punishment and disassociation, especially with other members that could be influenced.

Tamar was certainly put in a challenging position and only God could have vindicated her cause. She was stripped from the possible income of her deceased husband's home and lost out on her share of the wealth. She had no status or position except being a widow. The comfort of her security was removed from around and under her, with no contingency plan in place for her to redeem her position.

The false promise of Judah to give Tamar his last son, Shelah into marriage when he was old enough, was all she had to hold on to. She was not invited or welcomed within the family circle, as she was deemed to be the cause of the deaths of her two husbands; a matter which she had no insight in herself, as the Awesome God of Heaven and Earth was the only one who had determined the fate of the men.

The word of the Lord said: "My whole being will exclaim, Who is like you, O Lord? You rescue the poor from those too strong for them, the poor and needy from those who rob them." Psalm 35:10 NIV. There is nothing that is too hard for God to do.

Tamar's life, aspiration and dreams were in Judah's mind an action; frozen with no hope of thawing. She was put out to tread waters that she was incapable of managing. It must have felt like she had been placed into the wide sea, to keep on paddling with no return, to her dying days. Evidently, as Shelah was never going to realistically reach the age of consent for marriage to Tamar, this was a matter of fact in Judah's mind.

It is my view that you would marvel if you knew what others genuinely thought about you. In many cases, it is easier to think evil of others than good, because for the greater part, the nature of human beings is in many instances dishonest and self seeking! Thus, I believe that some rejoiced at Tamar's removal from the family home, while others pondered as to what exactly did happen.

LOOKING WITH ANTICIPATION

We all live in hope that the ambitions of our hearts would not be dashed but fulfilled. However, when the contract for fulfilment is deceptive, then as living beings we are left to develop personal ideals that will lead us to the desired promise. In Tamar's case the ambition was the desire to bring forth the royal seed; she is not giving up hope and why should she? It is stated: ..."For she saw that, though Shelah had now grown up, she had not been given to him as his wife." Genesis 38:14 NIV

Nothing will change until we are ready to activate change. The supremacy is with the Almighty God to help us. He said that: "I will go before you and will level the mountains; I will break down gates of bronze and cut through bars of iron. I will give you the treasures of darkness, riches stored in secret places, so that you may know that I am the Lord, the God of Israel, who summons you by name." Isaiah 45:2-3 NIV.

Like a prisoner, many people are held in captivity of various types. However, if you have the mind to escape and trust God without doubting Him, He has the strategy to spring you a deserving surprise of victory.

Tamar was placed in the position of a scapegoat by her father-in-law, Judah. This was a mean act, coming from a godly man, which was compounded by her being shunted from the household. Being blamed wrongly is a tall order to bear, even for the meekest of persons. Women, do let us lighten the burden by not being punitive to each other.

CHAPTER 4

<u>INTIMACY AND SEX</u>

In this life there are three things that are a must for human continuation, they are:

- The word of God to inspire the soul, cleanse the heart and enlighten the spirit.

- A variety of nutritional food to fill the stomach, energise the being and strengthen the body.

- Sex and intimacy to invigorate the sexual senses, propel the reproductive organs and bring new life into existence.

INTIMACY AND SEX

Understanding the feelings of Tamar, in her bewilderment and banishment, is not hard. Many times, our own selfishness and wickedness put a barrier between us being understanding and compassionate or being judgmental and vindictive in our dealings with others.

Intimacy is having the commitment, devotion, warmth, love and understanding to lavish upon the person we give ourselves to. Sex, on the other hand, is an act of expression that has its climax in erotic passion, which ultimately fulfils the creation plan of God for us to multiply.
The Lord has fixed it, so that the biological monthly cycle pushes the body to a peak and trough inclination.

Tamar, in her isolation, having a healthy mind, body and spirit had to no doubt adopt this saying: "…the God who gives life to the dead and calls things that are not as though they were." Romans 4:17 NIV

In assessing the quality of Tamar's sex life, it is my view that it had much to be desired. Deep down she wanted to fulfil her dream to bring forth the cluster associated with the meaning of her name, but the men she had were not up to the job. Lot's daughters said: .."Our father is old, and there is no man around here to lie with us, as is the custom all over the earth."

Genesis 19:...31 NIV

Sex and intimacy is very much a taboo subject in many Church organisations in this twenty first Century. Growing up and adhering to the commands, rules and regulations imposed on believers has definitely brought home the reality that may have laid the foundation to help restrict Tamar's movement at her father's place.

She could not be seen in public with anyone else, as she would be considered unfaithful to Judah's false promise.

It did not matter how much Tamar prayed, fasted, wept, worry or exercised all the physical, emotional and spiritual output she was able to display. Judah's mind was firmly made up, thus the only one that Tamar could turn to was the

Lord her Maker. Indeed turning to the Lord is the very best option available to us women.

The Lord cannot fail, lie or deal with us like mortals!

Tamar must have sensed her biological clock ticking away as she was older than Shelah, and so she wisely looked for an opportunity to turn the tables on Judah, by tricking him to have her as a prostitute in order to prove her innocence and to move herself on, and more importantly bring the royal seed into being.

It is my idea that God worked with Tamar and gave her His blessing, so that Judah would know that. …"The Lord does not look at the things man looks at. Man looks at the outward appearance, but the Lord looks at the heart."

1 Samuel 16:7 NIV

The Lord incited Judah to rise to the occasion of going in to the woman Judah believed to have been the temple prostitute. It states: "Where is the shrine-prostitute who was beside the road at Enaim? Genesis 38:21 NIV

God certainly has ways and means to get us to comply with His plan in order to bring us to His expected end. Although Tamar was ambitious to conceive, it was God who brought forth His plan into existence, or else the future would not have panned out for generations to come concerning the offspring of King David.

SUBJECTING THE BODY

Salaciously Tamar takes her place with those deemed less worthy in our society, 'prostitutes'. She had to change her mindset and outlook on life so that she could form a sure foundation for a brighter tomorrow.

Tamar must have played the scene of giving herself to Judah over and over again in her mind and could not see any other option available to her. I believe she prayed, hoped and anticipated but change was far away. The only way out was for her to take her place in the same arena as those who give their body for money.

Could Tamar possibly adopt a similar fear and inner groaning as Jesus did in the garden of Gethsemane, when He prayed and said? .."My Father, if it is possible, may this cup be taken from me. Yet not as I will, but as you will."
Matthew 26:..39 NIV

Many a time we are left alone to make some crucial decisions. It is at these moments that you and I understand ourselves best because inner determination, tenacity and courage have to come from within the inner part of our being to act in the best interest of our future care and welfare.

The Lord in His wisdom, helped to disguise Tamar's voice, aroused Judah's sexual desire and left him without the means to pay for the service he needed. Judah's friend was there but he could not assist. Therefore after Judah handed over the security needed by Tamar, Judah was able to take his best shot into her and ultimately shot his best two offspring.

I say to every woman, when doing the expected is not bringing the change, then by the leading of God, another method must be employed.

The true reason for the death of Judah's two sons was never revealed to anyone. God has ways of vindicating the defenceless causes and disclosing what is hidden. "There is nothing concealed that will not be disclosed, or hidden that will not be made known." Luke 12:2 NIV. Our Abba Father will take care of that private distress that you cannot mention to another for fear of reprisal.

God alone was interested in what Tamar was going through. Do not expect people who do not have any genuine interest in your pain and hurt to empathise with you. In fact, from experience, many would rejoice at the sign of misfortune happening to you due to their prejudices about you before the incident. The word of the Sovereign Lord then can only be our assurance and confidence. "I know that everything God does will endure for ever, nothing can be added to it and nothing taken from it. God does it so that men would revere Him." Ecclesiastes 3:14 NIV

CONCEPTION

The road to success and victory is filled with challenges. There are many hills and mountains to climb to get to the top; taking risks is a part of being transported into your destiny.

Judah abrogated his responsibility after copulating with Tamar. In order for Tamar to alter what was going on or not as the case might be, she had to develop the attitude of a risk taker and take the mental, sexual and physical challenge to change the way things had been for herself, since the death of her husbands.

Tamar asked for Judah's prized possessions and got them without him fussing: He asked, "What pledge should I give you?" "Your seal and its cord, and the staff in your hand," she answered. So he gave them to her and slept with her, and she became pregnant by him." Genesis 38:18 NIV

I question the irresponsibility of Judah, not to seek to use any protection. Also his lack of notion that he had during his time of ecstasy; that he had in fact made fertile the womb of Tamar, but I guess this is a matter that is too high for certain human beings to fathom, especially when personal need is the priority. 'The moment of self gratification is a sneaking impostor'. Thus, everyone has to be on the look out, less you will be caught in its trap!

To conceive a child/ren, ideas or any thing important, self must be subjected and denied and risks taken.
The initial experience of taking risk can be frightening and may make you feel tense; almost like a tight squeeze.
Perhaps it could be likened to that of a thread passing through the eye of a tiny needle. I am confident though in saying that God is pulling you through, painful though it may be!

CHAPTER 5

<u>UTIMATE SHAME</u>

There is no-one like the God of
Jeshurun, who rides on the
heaven to help you and on the
clouds in his majesty.

The eternal God is your refuge,
and underneath are the
everlasting arms. He will drive
out your enemy for you, saying,
"destroy him!"

Deuteronomy 33:26-27

ULTIMATE SHAME

Shame to me is like a foul smell that stench. The news of what happened is on everybody's lips. It has become the main topic of every conversation. People you know and those who you do not, could be in your vicinity, simply talking about you and have not a clue that you are the person in question.

The ultimate shame happens when your situation has been plastered everywhere for everyone to have an opinion about the matter.

Hear what the word of the Lord says: " About three months later Judah was told, "Your daughter-in-law Tamar is guilty of prostitution, and as a result she is now pregnant." "Judah said, "Bring her out and have her burned to death!"

"As she was being brought out, she sent a message to her father-in-law. "I am pregnant by the man who owns these," she said. "And she added, "See if you recognise whose seal and cord and staff these are." Genesis 38:24-25 NIV

The news of Tamar's pregnancy made her a target for public spectacle and reproach. Tamar was guilty on several accounts:

For playing the role of a prostitute
For committing incest with her father-in-law
and for deception as she deliberately deceived Judah.
Such crimes carry huge penalties which are usually exercised swiftly so as to stop the practice becoming an epidemic.

Judah denied his part of the crime, even though his friend knew of his involvement with a prostitute three month before. Judah also deliberately deceived Tamar in believing that when his last son Shelah was old enough that he would give him to be her husband.

The only qualified judge in Tamar's case that was able to judge the matter fairly was equally guilty.
God will never let those who trust in him and are seeking to carry out his plan, be permanently put to shame. " In you I trust, O my God. Do not let me be put to shame, nor let my enemies triumph over me." "No one whose hope is in you

will ever be put to shame, but they will be put to shame who are treacherous without excuse."

Psalm 25:2-3 NIV.

Pronouncing condemnation on those who we consider to be guilty, and sentencing them before trial can be damning, and the condemnation can have a knock on effect on ourselves, like Judah who was just as guilty as the accused Tamar.

I believe as brave as Tamar presented, as a normal mortal human being she must have felt certain parts of the body tightening up, nervous, racing fluttering heart beats and generally burdened down.

Shame has a way of infiltrating the most innocent of people, the meekest of individuals, kind and good-natured individuals. Its impact is and can be amazing because it comes as a total surprise to its target victim. Therefore, to not have impartial, fair- minded individuals judging the matter on your behalf, can be catastrophic and evidently compounds the problem.

Judah was not impartial in his initial handling of the news of Tamar's pregnancy, but he was honest in owning up to his sin in the matter of her being pregnant.

Judah displayed a unique quality that I believe is lacking in many men today and most worrying being in Christendom, seems to make very little difference to their behaviour. I know the scripture is our only genuine source of assurance and faith: "Do not gloat over me, my enemy! Though I have fallen, I will rise. Though I sit in darkness, the Lord will be my light.

Micah 7:8 NIV.

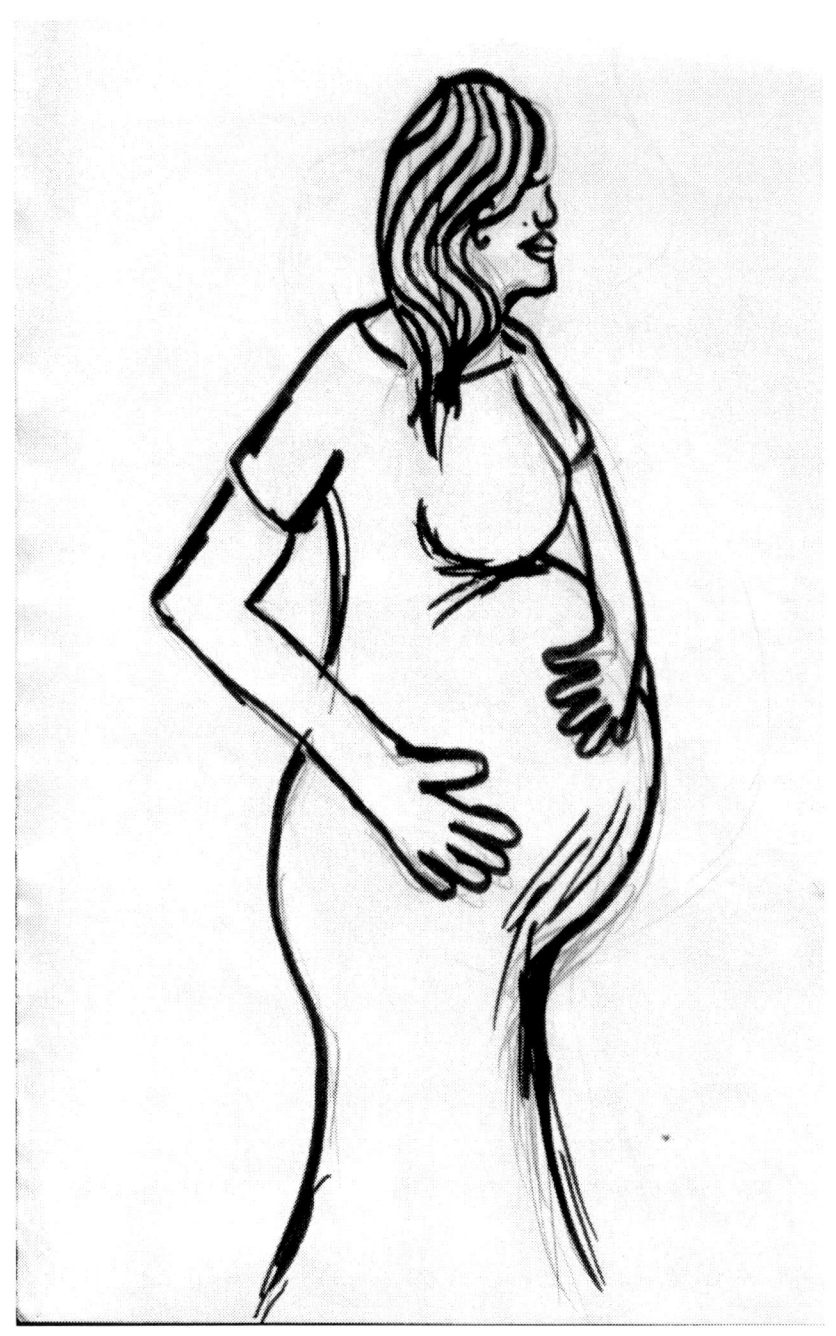

PREGNANCY

Whilst there are so many women yearning to become pregnant to continue the generation, there are those for whom it is their worse nightmare.

For Tamar it was a time of ecstasy in the realisation of the pregnancy, no doubt, as she was deemed incapable before this moment.

Many women are carrying years of hurt and pain because of becoming pregnant. They have been forced against their will to get rid of it and have since been living a life of guilt that will not go away.

Others have carried it but are not happy for the experience they went through. Whilst others like Tamar praise God for the chance it gave them to have their lives transformed.

Lot's daughters gave impetus to the joy of pregnancy. "So both of Lot's daughters became pregnant by their father. The older daughter had a son and she named him Moab; he is the father of the Moabites of today. The younger daughter also had a son, and she named him Ben-Ammi; he is the father of the Ammonites of today." Genesis 19: 36-38 NIV

The moral etiquette of sometimes our fanatic behaviour, could, if God was on an equal footing with us, obliterate His Will and purpose for many of our life's destiny.

Life itself is full of surprises, with or without our contribution. I encourage you therefore to embrace Christ Himself to lead, guide and instruct you in the way you are to go.
The Mighty God is the one that is able to defend you justly and raise you above your shame and pain.

On a different note and under a different circumstance, I can hear the encouraging word of Jesus to Simon. Perhaps you could put your name in the place of Simon, as this I believe is God's desire for us His children. "…….. ……… "Satan has asked to sift you as wheat. But I (Jesus) have prayed for you, …….that your faith may not fail. And when you have turned back, strengthen your sisters (brothers)."
St Luke 22:31-32 NIV
The truth of the matter is that someone has to go through that experience to assist others to be over-comers, and why not us? So, be the first to be equipped to lend a helping

hand. Let another bless God for you and your overcoming experience, which they can emulate. I am aware that this can of course single you out as a born leader and a fighter, but God has put certain innate abilities within you to do His exploits, for His praise, honour and renown working in you.

Pregnancy has its own ups and downs. The physical strain on the body is huge, therefore to carry the heavy burden of disgrace with it is enough to destroy you and destabilise your resolve to want to live.

Living cannot be a choice when you are going through difficulties. It has to be a must. The Spirit of the Lord is hovering over us saying: "I will not die but live, and will proclaim what the Lord has done." Psalm 118:17 NIV Dying undoubtedly is the easy way out; it is the road of quitters. If you are out of it, then there can be no more pain but you would certainly forfeit the joy that is awaiting the winners, which Christ will make you to be, as long as you trust His Lordship to Shepherd you.

BURN HER

The plea for the leader to take drastic action with dealing
with you and the willingness of others to make sure it is
done is in another sphere all by it self. The words of Judah
when he heard the news of Tamar's pregnancy was not to
privately ascertain what may have happened to her but to
demonstrate the authority invested in him to do something.
…"Judah said, bring her out and have her burned to death!"
Genesis 38:..24 NIV.

Observe carefully the shared silence and lack of concern
expressed by others. Is this familiar? Where was Judah's
servant who was with him when he stopped to have sex?
Where was the compassion of Tamar's leaders when they
heard of Tamar's plight and the threat of the death penalty
sanctioned for her? Where were the extended family
members, the brethren and wider community members?
We certainly don't need to ask where God was, because
even if you cannot find the right word to express to Him,
God is certainly always near.

The Lord is seeing the tears, He is hearing the groaning and He is a fair and Just God to all. So, for many watching you squirming in despair, agony and hopelessness, which may bring on a lasting thrill to their dull world, a word of caution needs to be in place.

The word of the Lord confirmed: "Not by might nor by power, but by My Spirit, says the Lord Almighty."

Zechariah 4:6 NIV

Human selfishness seems to take precedence when we don't understand a difficult matter and worse, if we are not fond of the person who is the victim. But let us take heed to our bad ways and shape up and hear the word of the Lord. "Do not take advantage of a widow or an orphan. If you do and they cry out to me, I will certainly hear their cry."

Exodus 22:22-23 NIV

So when you are viewed as the problem, judged and incarcerated by the masses, do not fall into the trap that is set for you to remain there; look and see the beautiful door set before you by the Lord for your escape and advancement. "I know your deeds. See, I have placed before you an open door that no-man can shut. I know that you have little strength, yet you have kept my words and have not denied my name." Revelation 3:8 NIV. It is the Lord alone that matters; so do not allow yourself to be phased by trials. They too will pass and you will see the glory of the Lord exalted through your life.

It is my experience that you cannot do anything about people who have hang ups about you, as each of us is responsible for the thought processes of our minds, and no one else's, even if we give others the power to dominate us and to bully us to accept their thinking on the issue. It is not cool to help destroy another person, neither is it going to benefit us to see them being ruined.

Women who have been burned by life's wicked attack and are struggling to make sense of how this could have happened to you, I want you to start taking control of your mind and seek God's face in earnestness to blot out the terrible memory that is a hindrance to your destiny. Rise and be healed and use the experience to help bring change to self and someone else's life.

Many individuals would like to witness you literally being burnt by the raging hatred and anger they are harbouring towards you.

They would like to see you burned by their prediction and plots for you!

Equally, they would like to see you burnt in the isolation they have been party to, by singling you out as a bad example, to have in existence living in the same Universe as them.

God's plan is to see you escape un-scorched. He demonstrated this in providing the means for Tamar to escape death by fire and He did so for the three Hebrew boys who were thrown into the fiery furnace.

Make every effort to escape every type of burning others would relish seeing you in. Escape with your faith intact and be confident in the assurance that your Heavenly Father's shepherding care is hovering over you for you deliverance and victory.

THE GREAT ACCLAIMED

Judah's acclaim towards Tamar was unplanned, he said:
"She is more righteous than I, since I wouldn't give her to
my son Shelah." Genesis 38:26 NIV. It is a blessing and
joy to know that life operates like the different weather or
the seasons. No two days are ever alike; life has a
metamorphic ability to transform situations instantaneously
around us for our good, as long as the situation is in the will
of God. "May those who seek my life be disgraced and put
to shame; may those who plot my ruin be turned back in
dismay." Psalm 35:4 NIV. Who could have foreseen that
Judah in his dogma would sentence Tamar and then
commission her to be burnt to death, or equally, that her
producing certain items as evidence could have annulled the
case in the midst of the spectating crowd? Observe
carefully that: "As she was being brought out, she sent a
message to her father-in-law." "I am pregnant by the man
who owns these," she said. And she added, "See if you
recognise whose seal and cord and staff these are." "Judah
recognised them…" Genesis 38:25-26 NIV

The recognition of the choice items was left for Judah's conscience and thanks be to God he acknowledged they were his and so he rightly promoted Tamar, beyond his own initial plan.

Many times we are put into some embarrassing predicaments and it does not help that there are those wishing and plotting our fall for no good reason, except they have concluded from their warped minds what they imagine is the problem and the sentence to be for you.

Our God however, has the power to take the tongues and tactics of your enemies and let them rightly announce the righteousness of God imprinted on you, amidst the injustice and scandals that are going around about you!

It is therefore imperative that you do not let your guard down, by opening up yourself, to accommodate the following unwelcome guests that have been outlined to your hurt. Do everything in your power to keep these beings at a distance:

FAULTFINDERS

GOSSIPERS

AUTHORITARIANS

LAW ENFORCERS

MOCKERS

HATERS

ACCUSERS

BUSIBODIES

Many of the listed backers above are there, to basically distract you from reaching your destiny and fulfilling your God given potential. "A righteous man may have many troubles, but the Lord delivers him from them all." Psalm 34:19 NIV.

The Lord will bless you to hear many of your enemies say;
'I've got it wrong'. Judah felt that he was squeaky clean,
holy and much more righteous than Tamar, but he was in
for a shock as truth confronted him and convicted him.

In the events leading up to the contest for righteousness
between Tamar and Judah, the condemned Tamar must
have felt at her wits end with sorrow and grief. Whilst Judah
felt comfortable, relaxed and assured that he was justified
both in his own eyes and in the eyes of the people around
him.

Consequently, only the Divine intervention of God Himself
could have exulted Tamar out of her distress and hurt. The
word of the Lord confirmed: "He raised the poor from the
dust and lifts the needy from the ash heap; He seats them
with princes, with the princes of their people."
 Psalm 113:7-8 NIV.

You may have been singled out to look bad and whilst you
are experiencing the trauma of the pain that this engendered,
seconds turn to minutes, minutes to hours, hours to days,

days to weeks, weeks to months, months to years and years to decay. The pressing weight of it all can prove hard to bear but do remember that the Lord is true to His promise to be with you always.

The cloud of the glory of the Lord is over you to guarantee you safety.

CHAPTER 6

<u>BARRENNES TO FRUITFULNESS</u>

All the trees of the field will know I the Lord bring down the tall trees and make the low trees grow tall. I dry up the green tree and make the dry tree flourish. "I the Lord have spoken, and I will do it."

Ezekiel 17:24 NIV

BARRENNESS

The inability to reproduce self is one that bears heavily on those who are not comfortable by this fate.

Man made barrenness must then be extremely difficult to cope with. Tamar was seemly barren, as she did not produce any children for neither of her two husbands as was expected. In fact, Onan was specifically told he should take Tamar as his wife and that he should raise up children for his deceased brother. Examine this verse carefully: "Then Judah said to Onan, "Lie with your brother's wife and fulfil your duty to her as a brother-in-law to produce offspring for your brother."
Genesis 38:8 NIV.

Barrenness is deemed as a curse in many cultures and in the religious sphere there is no exception. To then be subjected to this loathing curse can be very distressing and brings a level of disheartenment.

Many people can find themselves being very bitter and discouraged but I would like to say that the Lord has built in a safety net for all those who are experiencing a level of loneliness, sadness and grief due to un-productivity. The words expressed to Elisha whilst he was in Jericho concerning the natural land and its lack of usefulness and worth to the people of the land, states: "The men of the city said to Elisha, "Look, our lord, this town is well situated, as you can see, but the water is bad and the land is unproductive." "Bring me a new bowl," he said, "and put salt in it." So they brought it to him. Then he went out to the spring and threw the salt into it, saying, "This is what the Lord says: 'I have healed this water. Never again will it cause death or make the land unproductive.'" And the water has remained wholesome to this day, according to the word Elisha had spoken."

2Kings 2:19-22 NIV.

There are many points worth taking notice of in these verses, which can be used to compare the parameter for changing our mind set and embodying the plan God has for us.

The town is well situated - You are strategically situated to bring the necessary change needed.

The water is bad and the land is unproductive – You are feeling bad and not fulfilling your usefulness. Wake up; this is your moment to cut the umbilical cord of self-dependency and on others. Rise up and liberate yourself to be all that Christ has genetically blue printed for you to become.

The Sovereign Lord has a word for you.

Like the water and the land "I have healed you" Jesus is saying. Use your tongue positively to benefit your life: "The tongue has the power of life and death, and those who love it will eat its fruit." Proverbs 18:21 NIV.

There are too many children in the universe that are looking for attention, love, care and protection. They can be found in the family, in the schools, in the community, the sanctuary etc. Most importantly, some people's man-made barrenness needs to be broken. To break the latter certain perils must be overcome. Every positive embryonic idea can mushroom into that outstanding success you have been waiting for.

Our Abba Father in Heaven has not the ability to practice partiality. He cannot be influenced neither can He be forced against His will, like humans can be. The word of the Lord states: "For the Lord your God is God of gods and Lord of lords, the great God, Mighty and Awesome, who shows no partiality and accepts no bribes." Deuteronomy 10:17 NIV.

With total assurance then we can relax in the sure promises of the Lord that He will not leave us or forsake us but He will be with us always.

Jesus at His hour of being crucified, when the natural mind would be too perplexed and muddled, encouraged women in a profound manner, beyond human limited knowledge, wisdom and understanding: "A large number of people followed Him, including women who mourned and wailed for Him. Jesus turned and said to them, Daughters of Jerusalem, do not weep for me; weep for yourselves and for your children. For the time will come when you will say, 'Blessed are the barren women, the wombs that never bore and the breast that never nursed!"

St. Luke 23:27-29 NIV.

Of course the true meaning of these verses is to do with end time prophecy; it is nonetheless relevant to many barren women's situations today.

The paradox for Tamar was that she must have felt the innate intuition that she was a perfect, fruitful woman, waiting for the opportune moment to be impregnated. But the insidious innuendoes of Judah and the behaviour of others towards her, must have made her feel disgraced and certainly misplaced, a fatal mistake that too often we are guilty of being embedded in.

Like Jonah, many barren women are identifying with these sayings: "Now, O Lord take away my life, for it is better for me to die than to live." Jonah 4:3 NIV.

When has it ever been better to die than to live, even when in dire straights? The option to chose death rather than life and vice versa is not up to us.

Hurting women, God is our panacea, the perfect cure to all our heartaches. Let us wisely develop the ability to look at a matter from a parallax angle. In failing to do this, we could be paralysing each other to the pathetic detriment of our own selves.

A vivid account

Recently I caught the tail end of a TV wild life programme. I observed a pair of mating birds, (I am uncertain of its exact type). They set up home hewed out in the upper part of the tree. They nested three eggs and the dad to be fortified the incubating mum with her daily meals.

The eggs hatched at different periods. Mum blocked up the entrance to the home, leaving only a hole through which they would feed. The father bird kept to his responsibility in supplying his immediate family with daily food.

One of the chicks died early in its development, as it was not robust in positioning itself to snatch the food on father's arrival each time.

The other two chicks continued with mother hovering over them as carer and protector.

The time came when mother pecked her way out of the hole and left the two chicks in it to continue with their development. She joined father to supply them with more food, as the appetite of the chicks became more demanding.

On mother leaving the nest the stronger chick took charge and blocked up the hole, leaving a small hole to feed through. The stronger chick remained at the entrance of the hole and of course dominated the food supply on mother and father's arrival each time.

It's ferocious appetite put it in good stead to take on life in and beyond the nest.

The more robust chick grew strong, confident and courageous and so eventually it pecked its way out of the hole and flew the nest and started life as an independent, free willed, liberated bird. Though young and inexperienced, the young chick did what came naturally. The other young chick continued to be cared for by both parents. The parents kept encouraging it to venture out by their special communication skills of cooing it but to no avail.

This chick would not risk flying the nest. Subsequently, a few bees kept coming by, wanting to take up residency in the said hole. The chick put up a good fight in snapping up many of the bees until finally it was overrun by a swarm of bees, too much for the single chick to handle.

The chick lost its fight to live, as the swarm of bees destroyed it and took up residence of their choice place to manufacture their honey, as they were created to do.

Similarly, you can remain in that stagnated situation, feeling like trouble is constantly being a nuisance as it is ever hovering over you, discomforting you, threatening your dignity, self -worth, making you feel exhausted. Minute by minute you are feeling like you are dying slowly and generally you are feeling stunted, as you put up a good fight like the bird that would not leave, you are doing your best in pecking away at the problem only to find that the problem is bigger and more powerful than your ability to overcome it. Well, try and pull yourself together and reach out to your Maker. He is willing and able to change things for you. Christ is waiting for you to call Him, the escape route has already been worked out, and all you need to do, is to get ready to get out of that hole.

The morals for me in this anecdote are:

(1) You have to be determined to win against the probabilities, as there is intuitive potential invested in

all of us, to be the very best, just like it was in the robust chick that survived.

(2) You have to position yourself to fly the nest of complacency and soar to the unknown of God's utmost for you!

(3) You have got to know when staying a moment longer is detrimental to your existence. Don't be afraid, the earth is the Lord's and the fullness thereof. Step out, rise up and excel to God's highest for you.

As it is written: "Since ancient times no one has heard, no ear has perceived, no eye has seen any God besides you, who acts on the behalf of those who wait for Him" Isaiah 64:4 NIV.
Whatever is the undercurrent for your barrenness, be it physical, spiritual, financial, sexual, social emotional etc, let me reiterate forcefully that with God and in God, you can conquer triumphantly.

When the Lord God called unto Abraham and told him to look beyond his surroundings into the sky and view the great promise awaiting him and generations to come, the true heir was far from being in existence. "God took him outside and said, "Look up at the heavens and count the stars – if indeed you can count them." Then He said to him, "So shall your offspring be." Genesis 15:5 NIV. Abraham could not count the stars, our genius mathematicians cannot count them and neither can we!

Think outside of the box of limitation. Elisha using the salt to heal the land is a good analogy for barren women, as it shows that only God can alter the course of the barrenness you are experiencing and give you permanent healing and lasting joy with thanksgiving.

FRUITFULNESS

It is my belief that Tamar understood the meaning of her name, which is a cluster and or palm tree. Both meanings carry a bright future, so to then forfeit the chance to reproduce due to human obstacles would be suicidal for Tamar.

I equally believe that she had made up her mind that some way, somehow, by hook or by crook, she had to bear fruit and therefore fulfil her main purpose, as she perhaps frequently foresaw herself in her vision as a chosen mother. God has a way of revealing His mind and will to individuals before He brings them to pass.

The word of the Lord stated: "The secret things belong to the Lord our God, but the things revealed belong to us and to our children forever, that we may follow all the words of this law." Deuteronomy 29:29 NIV.

The Sovereign Lord helped Tamar in the plan conceived in her heart to ambush Judah to bring about the conception she had so desperately yearned for, by trapping Judah when she played the prostitute and when Judah sentenced her to be burnt to death. Thus Tamar perhaps echoed words similar to that which Elizabeth proclaimed to Mary: "In a loud voice she exclaimed; blessed are you among women, and blessed is the child you will bear." St Luke 1:42 NIV

The only wise God will not destroy the good plan He has reserved for our lifetime, for His honour and praise the Lord will bring to fruition that which has been foreordained for our good.

God reserved judgement as a last resort to turn our hearts to Him. He reads our hearts and knows our motives for doing what we do, when, how and with whom. "If you say, but we knew nothing about this, does not He who weighs the heart perceive it? Does not He who guards your life know it? Will He not repay each person according to what he has done?" Proverbs 24:12 NIV

The words from the Lord our maker is reassuring, and it is what generates hope and brings us into fruitfulness.

The display of fruitfulness gives joy, praise, excitement, richness and re-enforces God's favour on you. These examples can be found all around us; in farming, manufacture, in business, in child bearing, in extension of the family unit in fellowship, in increased wealth etc. It took God only three months to turn Tamar's future around: "About three months later Judah was told, "Your daughter-in-law Tamar is guilty of prostitution, and as a result she is now pregnant."

Genesis 38:24 NIV

It is amazing what God can do in three months. For years Tamar was deemed unfruitful. Now the Lord has turned her life around, removing sorrow, depression, hopelessness, dread, curse and so on. Here are additional cases displaying the wonder, good blessing and power of God to transpose the diligent into their rightful places.

"The ark of God remained with the family of Obed-Edom in his house for three months, and the Lord blessed his household and everything he had." 1 Chronocles13:14 NIV. Furthermore, David was immensely prosperous during the three months the ark of God was with Obed-Edom: "Now Hiram king of Tyre sent messengers to David, along with cedar logs, stonemasons and carpenters to build a palace for him. And David knew that the Lord had established him as king over Israel and that his kingdom had been highly exalted for the sake of His people Israel. In Jerusalem David took more wives and became the father of more sons and daughters. These are the names of the children born to him there: Shamua, Shobab, Nathan, Solomon, Ibhar, Elishua, Elpelet, Nogah, Nepheg, Japhia, Elishama, Beeliada and Eliphelet." 1 Chronicles 14:1-7 NIV.

In addition verses 15 & 17 of the said chapter above states: "As soon as you hear the sound of marching in the tops of the balsam trees, move out to battle, because that will mean God has gone out in front of you to strike the Philistine army, all the way from Gibeon to Gezer." " So David's fame spread throughout every land, and the Lord made all the nations fear him."

Thus, David's royal home was built. He had a large family increase and was very successful in warfare.

With outstretched hands and gratitude of heart, I say yes to the multiple fruitfulness of God for you and me. Surely what God has done for Tamar in impregnating her, for

Obed-Edom's household and David in such a short space of time, He will undoubtedly do this and more for those of us who will take Him at His word and good promise.

Tamar has now attracted the change that is everlasting. Not long from now she will be experiencing the real joy of having children around her. Obed-Edom will experience the joy of wealth and David the multiple joys of having a royal palace, a whole cluster of children and supremacy in warfare over Israel's enemies and above all, fame that will cause others to fear and be in reverence, because God was with them, as He is with us today, if we will only trust and obey His word.

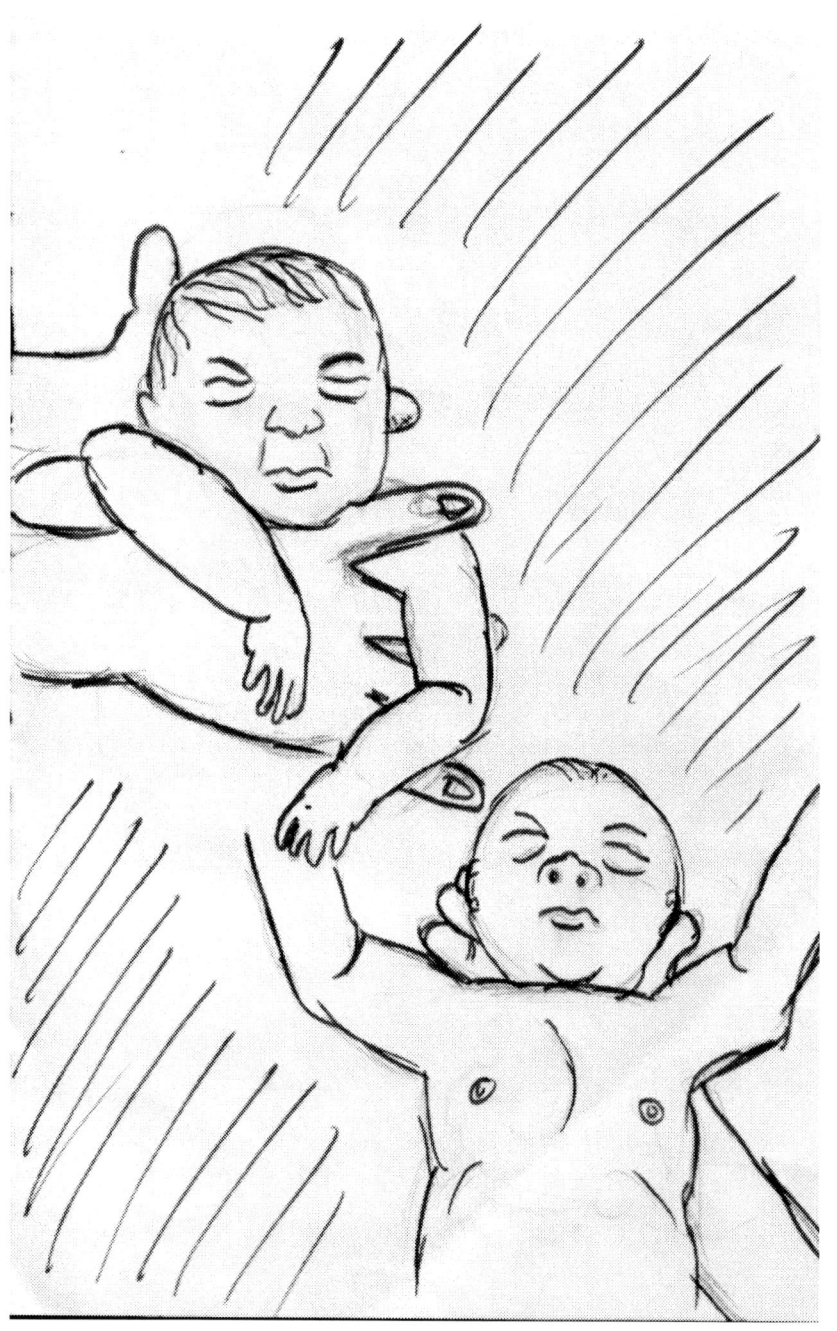

GIVING BIRTH AND BREAKING FORTH

At the time of giving birth, apart from the sheer discomfort, pain and anxiety for both mother and the unborn, it is also the time of anticipated exuberance.

"As Tamar was giving birth, one of the baby put out his hand; so the midwife took a scarlet thread and tied it on his wrist and said, "This one came out first." But when he drew back his hand, his brother came out, and she said, "So this is how you have broken out!" And he was named Perez. Then his brother who had the scarlet thread on his wrist came and he was given the name Zerah." Genesis 38:28-30 NIV

The mysterious hand of God did the unthinkable at the vulnerable stage of Tamar's life path. The hand of God did the illogical, the inconceivable and the most incredible deed for the midwife to behold.

The action displayed for the midwife to see was dangerous and the presentation of the hand of a child to be born was abnormal and perhaps frightening too.

Nevertheless, there is a time for everything under the sun, and this was certainly the time for the midwife to bear witness that this birth was not ordinary, and neither was the children coming literally through the seemingly, once barren womb of Tamar.

"Praise be to the Lord God, the God of Israel, who alone does marvellous deeds."

Psalm 72:18 NIV.

In our world of soap opera, I can almost hear the thumping beat of the music rising as the drama of shock, disbelief, the racing of the heart beats, impels its waiting audience to dare to make any comment, except to reiterate the mystery of it all.

The messy and embarrassing rough route of the past blame, shame and disgrace Tamar went through cannot be compared to the ecstasy she was about to bask in. I perceived that Tamar had to alter her mindset as well as her circle of confidantes, if she had any!

With the courage and grace of God within Tamar, she took the risk needed to give birth; she faced a barrage of criticism and discomfort of the pregnancy. She subdued herself to the wailing and the panting process. I consider that Tamar may have had to anaesthetise her emotions, her mind, her body and spirit in order to pull herself up and out of the predicament of non-progress she found herself in. She placed herself with the help and blessing of God in a perpetuated situation in order to live forever.

The word of the Lord said: "A woman giving birth to a child has pain because her time has come; but when her baby is born she forgets the anguish because of her joy that a child is born into the world." St. John 16:21 NIV

The question I would like to ask you, is there anything that you can do right now to bring your self into transformation?

It is said that procrastination is the thief of our time, therefore make concrete positive plans to take action today. Yes, it is a challenge, but how do you eat an elephant? 'one bite at a time'. Break through demands for us to take one step at a time and one day at a time. The journey to the top of the mountain is always and must always begin with that single step and each step will take you to your aspired goal, especially if you include the supernatural help of the Lord, which states: "In all your ways acknowledge Him, and He will make your path straight."

Proverbs 3:6 NIV

Years have gone by and nothing important has been accomplished, as it was for Tamar so it is for many hurting women. Now is the pivotal moment to embark upon your journey, which may be isolated and lonely but for your destiny it has to be done. Don't be naïve in thinking that it will happen by itself. If you want it desperately enough, then go and get it. It is written: "In the same way, faith by itself, if it is not accompanied by action, is dead."

James 2:17 NIV.

Fittingly also: "The living, the living – they praise you, as I am doing today; fathers (mothers) tell their children' about your faithfulness."

Isaiah 38:19 NIV.

Remember that dignity, self worth, self-esteem have to be put on hold until giving birth is finished!

The moment of reality for countless hurting women is that estrangement has to come to an end. The rift engendered by tormentors has to have an abrupt completion. Take the power you have invested in those treating you less than an equal human being and break forth in the awesome name of Jesus. God stirred a miracle for Tamar and her offspring, now He is on red alert to help you. So are you ready? Like bungee jumping, your mind has to be ready for the plunge. Yes, the fear is surrounding you and threatening your stability but the truth is, you are the master of that fear and not the fear the master of you. Take control and don't forget the Lord has given us the power to go further and that is to take dominion!

NAMES TO BE RECKONED WITH

In every culture names are used to identify individuals but more importantly names are given in representation of the thoughts and feelings of the parents towards that child. In the canon of recorded scriptures, very few second names are attached to an individual, therefore the Christian name, as we know it to be, is of prime importance.

Observations are made, especially in the religious sphere that many fathers give their sons their own Christian names or the Grandparent's names or that of other significant individuals.

Here is a good example: "On the eighth day they came to circumcise the child, and they were going to name him after his father Zechariah, but his mother spoke up and said " No! He is to be called John" they said to her, " there is no one among your relatives who has that name." Then they made signs to his father, to find out what he would like to name the child. He asked for a writing tablet, and to everyone's astonishment he wrote, "His name is John." Immediately his mouth was opened and his tongue was loosed, and he began to speak, praising God. The neighbours were all filled with awe, and throughout the hill country of Judea people were talking about all these things. Everyone who heard this wondered about it, asking, "What then is this child going to be? "For the Lord's hand was with him"

St Luke1:59 -66 NIV

The names of the children Tamar bore were not known prior to their arrival in the universe. "But when he drew back his hand his brother came out, and she said, "so this is how you have broken out!" and he was named Perez (Pharez, Parez or Phares). Then his brother who had the scarlet thread on his wrist came and he was given the name Zerah."

Genesis 38:28-30 NIV

These two boys' names changed the destiny for their mother Tamar and set the stage for kings and ultimately for the Lord Jesus Christ, to come through this genealogy.

Perez, the first born of the twins, his name means 'breach' or 'break forth.' Of course he broke forth, causing the alienation of his mother Tamar to be abolished. God in His greatness, authority and being a just God did so at the arrival of Perez, to signify His approval of Perez and blessing and intervention upon Tamar, removing from her life every curse, abandonment, and suspicion, as He had not done with any other child in the universe, before Perez and after him.

His brother Zerah means 'splendour.' He was also given an outstanding name for generations to come.

Here is a list of important Biblical names and their Meanings;

Asher – Happy Gen 30:13

Benoni – Son of sorrow Gen 35:18

Eliezer – God is my Help Exodus 18: 4

Ephraim – Fruitful Gen 41:52

Eve – Life Gen 3:20

Gad – Fortune Gen 30:11

Issachar – Reward Gen 30:18

Judah – Praise Gen 29:35

Mara – Bitter Ruth 1:20

Have you ever asked yourself why parents do not name their child: Jezebel or Judas!

Other important names with their meanings:

Dorothy – Gift of God

Danielle – (Daniel) God is my judge: Daniel 1:3

Othnielle – (Othniel) Lion of God, God is might:
Joshua 15:17-18

Mary – The Perfect one or Bitter

Sharon – Fertile Princess

Dorcas - Gazelle – A woman who abounds in good deeds
and gifts of mercy.

I recall some years ago a pregnant case I was responsible for, and on the birth of the child, I asked the mother for the chosen name identified for him and she gave me a name that sounded okay. I further enquired as to the significance of it and its meaning: To my amazement as 'posh' as the name sounded, it was derived from the machine installed in the room to help monitor the baby's heart rate!

Many people are going around dissatisfied with their names. Many references are noted in the Bible of individuals whose names have been changed because of its negative connotation.

What is your name saying about you and have you taken on a name that has not a bright future?

It is important that you have a name that will not be blotted out: "May his descendants be cut off, their names blotted out from the next generation."

Psalm 109:13 NIV.

Perez's name infiltrated generations to follow: The meaning of his name is powerful, it is meaningful and of great significance, to this very day.

The tribe of Judah, to which Perez, Zerah and Shelah had their foundation, has been a great name of dominance and importance. Here is a list of scriptures that have connected Perez as the main embodiment.

Genesis 46: 12

Numbers 26: 20 - 22

1st Chronicles 2:4 – 5

Nehemiah 11: 4

Ruth 4:1- 11

Matthew 1:3

Luke 3:33

The tribe of Judah is one of the main patriarchal units within the history of Jacob's twelve sons and of Israel as a nation. Prior to Jacob's departure he blessed his sons and their offspring plus generations to come; this is what he had to say:

"Judah, your brothers will praise you; your hand will be on the neck of enemies; your father's sons will bow down to you. You are a lion's cub, O Judah; you return from the prey, my son. Like a lion he crouches and lies down, like a lioness – who dares to rouse him? The sceptre will not depart from Judah, nor the ruler's staff from between his feet, until he comes to whom it belongs and the obedience of the nations is his. He will tether his donkey to a vine, his colt to the choicest branch; he will wash his garment in wine, his robes in the blood of grapes. His eyes will be darker than wine, his teeth whiter than milk."

Genesis 49:8-12 NIV

The fixed blessings placed upon Judah are:

- Your brothers will bow down to you
- You are a lion cub – symbol of courage, strength and sovereignty.
- Pictured as a lion – Lion of the tribe of Judah
- The sceptre will not depart – Jesus the promised Messiah is the permanent sceptre/word.
- Tether donkey to vine and colt to the choicest branch. Judah's descendants will one day enjoy a prosperous lifestyle and settle down.

These blessings pronounced by Jacob before his death, were not to be revoked or altered.

How marvellous to have a parent speaking positively into your life for generations to come.

It must be noted that not all the words said over the twelve sons were as empowering.

Every effort must be made by us to ensure that words of life, victory, strength, encouragement, praise etc, are grafted into our children's lives and those that we are having fellowship with, so as to emulate the plan of God.

You can change things for your generation and beyond.

What is your name saying about you? The Lord can make everything about you and your life new!

CLINCHING THE INHERITANCE

Tamar was no doubt living a life of destitution and certainly poverty stricken. She had no husband to provide for her general welfare. In fact she was stripped from the very right to remain in the home of her deceased husbands. Her future was bleak and troubled.

Women faired worse than men when they were left as widowed in Biblical culture. In Numbers 27:1-11NIV a wife is given no share of her husband's estate, as was the case of Tamar. Daughters and widows got a raw deal. From the different cultures and religious groupings, the law within the Quran caters more readily for all members of the family, in the event of death.

The first sign of the Biblical inheritance law being challenged was when the daughters of Zelophehad took what they saw as an unfair law, in practice to Moses, the elders and the congregation that had come together. Their names were: "Mahlah, Noah, Hoglah, Milglah, Milcah and Tirzah; they approached the entrance to the tent. 'So Moses brought their case before the Lord and the Lord said to him,

What Zelophehad's daughters are saying is right. You must certainly give them property as an inheritance among their father's relatives and give their father's inheritance over to them." Numbers 27:5-7 NIV

Women, God is just and fair in His dealings every time. Thank God for Moses who did not seek human consensus, instead he went directly to God for the answer. Lack of God's involvement in our affairs will leave us feeling unjustly treated, frustrated, hard done by, etc.

"The law of the Lord is perfect, reviving the soul. The statutes of the Lord are trustworthy, making wise the simple. The precepts of the Lord are right, giving joy to the heart. The commands of the Lord are radiant, giving light to the eyes. The fear of the Lord is pure, enduring forever. The ordinances of the Lord are sure and altogether righteous. They are more precious than gold, than much pure gold; they are sweeter than honey, than honey from the comb." Psalms 19: 7-10 NIV

The Lord is on the side of those who are hurting. Countless times He is trying to audibly tell us let not your heart be troubled, only believe in God and of course we think we know better, so we set off to do things our way, only to fail and have to start all over again.

The inheritance may be unfairly administered as in my case at the death of my dad. I am the only biological child for him and yet I stood outside looking on, as I watched my stepmother and her only child clinch everything, barring the pittance she sent me through the post without engaging me in any discussion on the matter of my dad's estate. I know my dad left a handsome amount, but I dare not venture there, as I have been held in an ostracised position for years.

I know of my dad's estate because he told me and regrettably he did not reveal to me any will that he had made. Not making a will is a disease that is rampant in my culture, as many of my parents' generation do not see the need to make a will. Equally, I have not been told of any will or provision left by him for either his grandchildren or myself.

Now I am aware that I could take the matter to the law of the land and get them to decide its outcome. I sense a notion though that my commitment within the church is viewed by them as one of naivety and that as I am serving God I should not be expected to be treated with any dignity or care 'because God is ultimately my inheritance'.

Also, this woman is so comfortable in taking liberties with me as his only child that it would be out of character for her not to continue doing so. The manipulation she exercised over him has been intense during the lifetime they spent together but only because he wanted it to be so.

He loved her and did everything to accommodate her wishes, feelings and her general welfare and at no time did I ever say anything about what I witnessed or perceived was the case. I lived among them as a peacemaker.

You and I don't have to do a thing more than pray, the all seeing, all knowing, powerful, wise God is in control and He has gone ahead to show His just working on our behalf.

"But you are a shield around me, O Lord; you bestow glory on me and lift up my head." Psalm 3:3 NIV.

Clinching the inheritance bestowed by the Almighty is my goal, as this is not perishable. I saw the way God called my dad home swiftly.
He did not enjoy his hard labour, he stayed as a watchman in the house, working constantly around the clock, accumulating wealth and extending the home, which neither he nor his offspring ever benefited from.

The example you have read about may never be able to compare with your saddened inheritance situation. You may have felt hard done by and are fretful about the situation. Hear the word of the Lord: "What good is it for a man to gain the whole world, yet forfeit his soul? Or what can a man give in exchange for his soul.
St Mark 8:36-37 NIV

Tamar and the children she bore clinched the inheritance held by Judah. They rose magically to a destiny that none could claim that they had assisted them to achieve.

God is our Abba Father. He has a sure inheritance awaiting us and more profoundly He is waiting for us. Therefore throw off the infuriation your emotion is caught up in and experience the freedom of God's peace, health, joy, loving-kindness, wealth, daily care and bountiful provision.

I feel confident and assured that through the Divine help of God and the unfeigned faith invested to bring the name of the Lord glory, that our inheritance is sure in this life and in the one to come. Also soon and very soon, you will look back and laugh in amazement at the goodness of God on your life. "The One enthroned in the heaven laughs; the Lord scoffs at them."

Psalm 2:4 NIV

CHAPTER 7

<u>FAME AND PROMOTION</u>

No-one from the East or the West or from the Desert can exalt a man. But it is God who judges: He brings one down, He exalts another.

Psalm 75:6-7 NIV

FAME AND PROMOTION

Hitting the headlines for the right reasons is what all human desire. No one wants to be singled out or to be made a poor example of.

Tamar was definitely famous and justly promoted. She endangered herself to move out and move on. The story of Judah throughout generations has confirmed her importance as being the cog in the wheel.

The Lord God told King David: "Now then, tell my servant David, this is what the Lord Almighty says: I took you from the pasture and from following the flock to be ruler over my people Israel. I have been with you wherever you have gone, and I have cut off your enemies from before you. Now I will make your name great, like the names of the greatest men of the earth."

2 Samuel 7:8-9 NIV

How magnificent is the power of God to take an individual from absolutely nowhere, no status, not from the 'upper class' and place them in the elitist bracket across the universe. Don't let your poor background and unsavoury beginnings hinder you! Can you try and analyse the sheer magic that is inherent in serving and trusting the Lord.

One moment David was following the sheep as their provider, protector and shepherd and the next moment he was on the royal throne as the great King of Israel. For many centuries following, David and his offspring dominated the royal throne. This eventually rippled into the arrival of the Sovereign Lord Jesus Christ, who is now reigning on the throne of David, as King, Prophet and Priest. David's prominence and reign, through the Lordship of Christ within him, resembled that of King Melchizedek: "The Lord has sworn and will not change His mind." "You are a priest forever, in the order of Melchizedek."

Psalm 110:4 NIV

God wants to take you out and to take you up into the unbelievable. So are you ready to follow the path of dignity, diligently? The great, great, great grandson of Tamar, the son of David, King Solomon by name, has been one of the world's greatest beings. The Queen of Sheba thought that she was the most eligible person to properly assess Solomon's fame and promotion.

Listed is her account: "When the queen of Sheba heard of Solomon's fame, she came to Jerusalem to test him with hard questions. Arriving with a very great caravan-with camel carrying spices, large quantities of gold, and precious stones-she came to Solomon and talked with him about all she had on her mind. Solomon answered all her questions; nothing was too hard for him to explain to her.

When the queen of Sheba saw the Wisdom of Solomon, as well as the palace he had built, the food on his table, the seating of his officials, the attending servants in their robes, the cupbearers in their robes and the burnt offerings he made at the temple of the Lord, she was overwhelmed."

She said to the King, "The report I heard in my own country about your achievements and your wisdom is true. But I did not believe what they had said until I came and saw with my own eyes.

Indeed, not even half the greatness of your wisdom was told me; you have far exceeded the report I heard."

2 Chronicles 9:1-6 NIV

I am optimistic that this is not just the experience of the late King Solomon, but that it can be for everyone who has entrusted their lives into the Mighty hand of God. Like the rain, the different weather, night and day, death and birth, bad and good experiences, have been allotted to every human being, irrespective of their background, race, creed, class, status and so on, so is the reality of God working for us and through us, to bring us into His best.

Good episodes are the delights of the soul. Here is a list of those who triumphed, whose gloom turned to happiness. They are:

Tamar – From low life to high life

Genesis 38, Ruth 4, 1Chronicles 2 & Matt.1:3

David – From following sheep to King of Israel

1st Samuels 16 & 17, 2nd Samuels 2 & 5

Jabez – From Sorrow and failure to utter success

1st Chronicles 4:9

Mephibosheth – From destitution and barrenness to being exalted, to the King's table.

2nd Samuels 9

The woman with the bleeding - to permanent health.

Matthew 9:20

Lepers – Scarred, disfigured bodies - to smooth cured bodies.

St Luke 17:11-19

Abraham's daughter – From being bowed down to being raised upright.

1st Samuels 2:8 & Luke 13:10-17

How do you see your position and what do you think the possibilities are for God to change it for you?

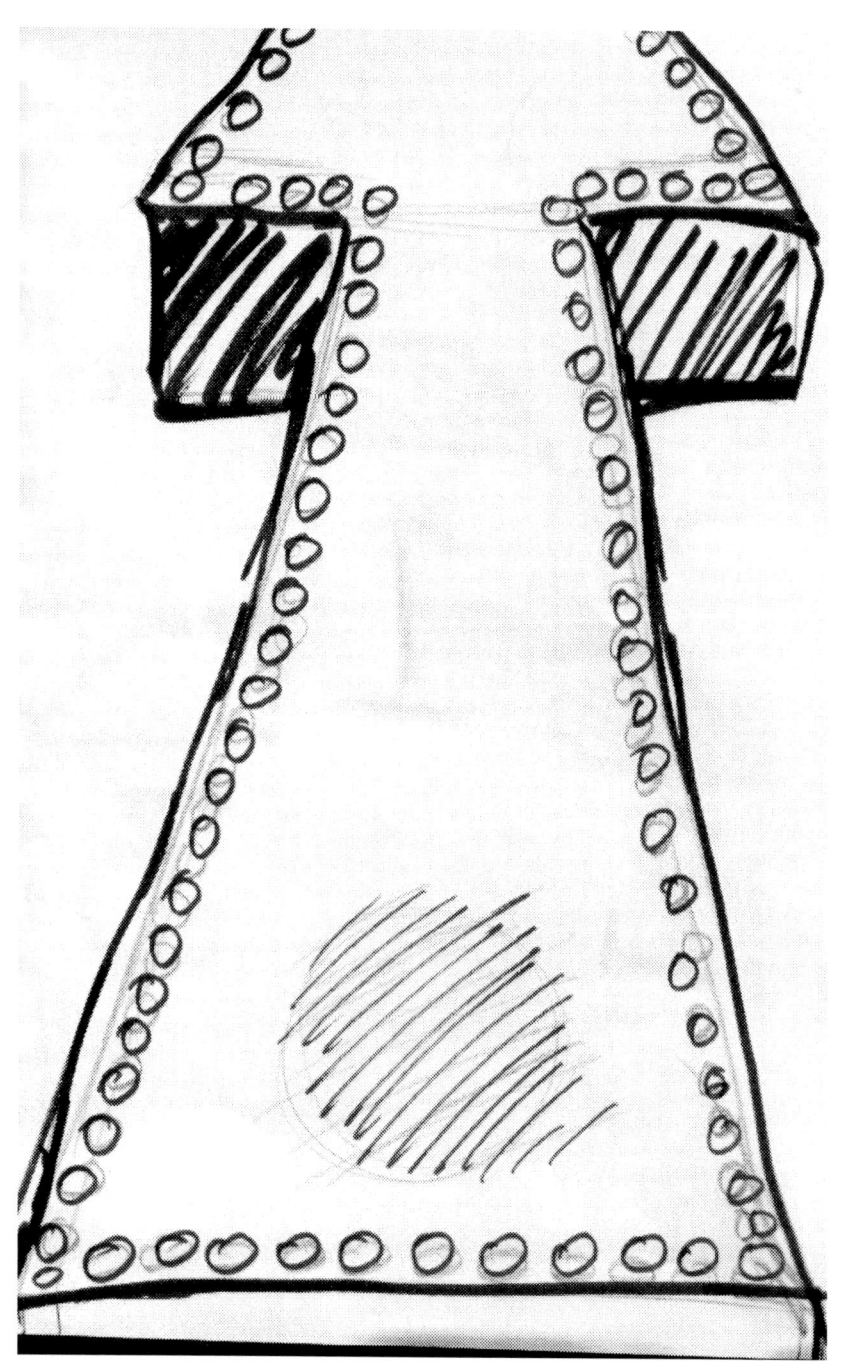

WALK THE ROAD OF ROYALTY

Tamar's journey from the time of her marriages to the time
of playing the prostitute, had been a torturous one,
uncertainties had ruled the day. She was put aside and was
surrounded by despair. She took matters into her own hands
and at the Mercy of God's loving-kindness she took a risk
that produced superb fruits. With the wisdom of God she
advanced her self-importance, rose to her rightful position
and excelled into monarchy.

This was very much equivalent to those stories with happy
endings. Tamar knew that if she was going to change her
status, she would need to change her focus. She broke the
mould of fear, dread and hopelessness. At no time in the
story of both Tamar and Judah, had the Sovereign Lord
made any reference that Tamar had dishonoured Him by
violating His will. We read though that God killed both Er
and Onan because they were wicked in His eyes and
obviously violated God's will.

She exalted Judah in ways that he had no prior understanding of what could have happened to him and his future in generations to come. The blessings that came upon Judah throughout all future generations was because of Tamar's action.

Secretly I believe that she warmed her faith, heart and spirit at the feet of the Sovereign Lord, the great God of Israel. The Lord said: "I will go before you and will level the mountain; I will break down gates of bronze and cut through bars of iron. I will give you the treasures of darkness, riches stored in secret places, so that you may know that I am the Lord, the God of Israel, who summons you by name."
Isaiah 45:2-3 NIV.

To find yourself at the top and not at the bottom is an incredible feeling. At last, Tamar is mingling with the world's greatest; she is no longer scorned, despised or dejected, but highly respected, praised and esteemed. "Charm is deceptive, and beauty is fleeting; but a woman who fears the Lord is to be praised. Give her the reward she has earned, and let her works bring her praise at the city gate." Proverbs 31: 30-31 NIV

Tamar is viewed in the eyes of the elders and leaders as a woman now of class and value. How wonderful it is to embrace celebrity. The word of the elders proclaimed over the lives of Boaz and Ruth, gives credence to the life of Tamar and to one of her sons: "Through the offspring the Lord gives you by this young woman, may your family be like that of Perez, whom Tamar bore to Judah. So Boaz took Ruth and she became his wife. Then he went to her, and the Lord enabled her to conceive, and she gave birth to a son. The woman said to Naomi: "Praise be to the Lord, who this day has not left you without a kinsman- redeemer. May he become famous through Israel! He will renew your life and sustain you in your old age. For your daughter-in-law who loves you and who is better to you than seven sons, has given him birth." Ruth 4:12-15 NIV

This, then, is the family of Perez:

Perez was the father of Hezron,

Hezron the father of Ram,

Ram the father of Amminadab,

Amminadab the father of Nahshon,

Nahshon the father of Salmon

Salmon the father of Boaz,

Boaz the father of Obed,

Obed the father of Jesse,

And Jesse the father of David

This genealogy has a list of ten great men who stemmed from Perez, showing the unique path that Tamar has paved the way for countless others to come through. Thus, Tamar has walked in the path of aristocracy and monarchy and this, thankfully, can only advance even higher for the servants of God.

Whatever you do, endeavour not to get caught up with meaningless fighting. Put your energy into seeking the face of the Lord, for your true advancement.

On examining the positions held by the then army divisions, look at who is at the head: "In charge of the first division, for the first month, was Jashobeam son of Zabdiel. There were 24,000 men in his division. He was a descendant of

Perez and chief of all the army officers for the first month."
1 Chronicles 27:2-3 NIV. Can you see yourself as the head? This is your moment to witness God's ability to raise you up! Like a learner swimmer, let yourself go by faith into the hand of God and witness His power to help you.

Life's turbulent storms that many of us have been caught up in, have happened to push us higher than our contemporaries. Let us develop the attributes of an eagle and ride the storms that have come to destroy us. Let us use the experience advantageously and not allow it to overtake our resilience to win. Whatever you do, try not to lie down and give up. With the fragment of strength left within you, I beseech you by the Divine help of God to get up and try and give your Maker the deserving privilege to stand by you!

Stepping into the spotlight of royalty demands that special attention is paid to every part of personal self and function. Therefore take dominion over the spirit of negativity and lack of motivation. Place yourself in the frame of mind as that of Queen Esther (Esther Chapter 2 NIV), take on a virgin mind set, virgin spirit and virgin persona. Sandwich these qualities with the entreating favour of the Lord. The result has to be success unlimited.

No one can hurt you as deeply as you hurt yourself. Don't give others the opportunity to take advantage of you. Your life is in you, for the glory, honour, praise and victory of the Lord who has, His blue print embedded within you. Weakness, failure, feebleness and inadequacies are not your potion because God who is for you, is with you, and He will guarantee your prosperity, as long as you make Him your Lord, Shepherd and Saviour.

EXCEL INTO THE HALL OF FAME

I used to visit Madam Tussauds in London annually. I was always fascinated by those deemed important enough to have a place in this museum. I observed the removal of the then Princess of Wales and her isolation from the royal family members group. Very old Monarchs were just as important as the current ones. The Princess though was less fortunate in her importance, especially at the time of her death, coupled with the revelations she gave prior to the fatal accident. This had made her a target for public derision.

Of course the decision to remove her and place her in isolation was administered by the powerful decision makers who decide who stays and who goes. What I am drawing on is the way we function even after a person is no longer in the place they once occupied. If we have it in for them they cannot escape our undying wrath without mercy. Only God can secure a place for us in the hall of fame without bias or prejudice.

Tamar can never again be put into the position that Judah once placed her in. She has by the Divine help of God, graduated into a prominent and progressive person with an imperishable future. See Ruth 4:18-22 NIV

In the genealogy of Jesus Christ, the bona fide status of Tamar is established: "Judah the father of Perez and Zerah, whose mother was Tamar." Matthew 1:3 NIV. Amazingly, there is no mention of Shelah, the surviving son of Judah and his wife Shua.

It is testimonies like Tamar's that gives credence to my faith in God that no matter how dismal a situation at present; it can change if you and I trust God and His word to deliver us!

Jesus, in His earthly ministry, made a keen observation of a woman who was hurting with a symptom of twelve years uncontrollable bleeding. He told her personally, after she made the effort to touch His garment: "Take heart, daughter," He said, "Your faith has healed you." And the woman was healed from that moment."

Matthew 9:22 NIV

Jesus is looking for no fame or gain for Himself; in fact it gives God pleasure to transform our lives to a quality and meaningful one. The problem is always with us obstructing the hand and movement of God: "Then should not this woman, a daughter of Abraham, whom Satan has kept bound for eighteen long years, be set free on the Sabbath day from what bound her?" "When He said this, all His opponents were humiliated, but the people were delighted with all the wonderful things He was doing."

St. Luke 13:16-17 NIV.

The Sovereign Lord wants to do some wonderful things for you in like manner. He is not afraid to take on the mobs, fight the battle for you and land you into victory. Because the Earth belongs to the Lord and everything in it and He has the power to demote or exalt whoever He chooses, Christ will give you inner power to stay delivered: "I will give you the keys of the kingdom of heaven; whatever you bind on earth will be bound in heaven, and whatever you loose on earth will be loosed in heaven."

Matthew 16:19 NIV.

There is a hidden Tamar's backbone enveloped in every hurting woman. Consequently, I encourage you to be very courageous and step out and form a lasting bridge between you and the Lord. Put your faith, trust and willingness in praying to the Lord and acting on His instructions. This, undoubtedly, will form a guarantee contract of His unfailing good promises, which will come to pass.

Take on the royal regalia prescribed for you by the Lord. The necessary bodyguards are standing to your attention. They are the angels of God that are assigned to protect you in your daily affairs.

The invisible presence of God will maximise your true value and worth. The Holy Spirit will endorse God's Will for you and now it is time for you to display that you can competently rise and maintain your high prestigious position.

HANDLING MISFORTUNE

Unless you have experienced misfortune at a time when you least expect it, it is hard to conceive the dispirited impact this has on the heart. Many people who have not experienced God have turned to substitute remedies, like anti-depressants, drinks, drugs and so forth. Some have lost their faith and the stamina to go on living, and have not been able to trust any source, visible or invisible.

The tool of contingencies is only effective if you know a thing is going to happen. Thanks be to God, He is a faithful Shepherd, who reveals the hidden things of darkness to His children. Many times this is not immediate but wait for it: "Therefore judge nothing before the appointed time; wait till the Lord comes. He will bring to light what is hidden in darkness and will expose the motives of men's hearts. At that time each will receive his praise from God."
1 Corinthians 4: 5 NIV

Take actions that will propel you to handle the challenges you are facing. Dry up your tears. Start taking care of number One. Try and keep your focus by meditating on the word of the Lord as documented in the Bible.

Don't wallow in self-pity. Avoid pity parties at all cost; they will only give permission for others to keep you captive in that position.

Align yourself with newness and freshness.

Say less, pray more and deepen your faith.

The spirits of critics will be evident as more and more people distance themselves from you. Years of good work would be wiped out like falling share prices. From my personal experience, it would feel like you have never done a good day's deed. Many will personally and ignorantly gloat over you! Whatever you do, avoid becoming discouraged or despondent, as this would lay a fertile ground for the enemy of your life to take advantage of your mind and function. Beseech the Lord to forgive those that are giving impetus to the devil and his evil to attack. From my experience many will literally hate you, talk badly about you and will lay burdensome oppression and guilt on you, if you grant them permission to do so.

Get ready to take charge. Go to the place where Tamar pulled herself up to. Begin to take charge and don't worry about the unknown. Keep your concentration on the known. As long as Tamar remained in her father's house unmotivated, just looking and anticipating, nothing would have changed. The piecemeal, lame promise of Judah was just enough to take her to her grave and no further.

But I hear the word of the Lord saying: "Open my eyes that I may see wonderful things in your law."

Psalm 119:18 NIV.

Equally, David has a word of further encouragement for all who are saddened: "May the table set before them become a snare; may it become retribution and a trap."

Psalm 69:22 NIV.

It is the power of these scriptures that gives me power to become an over comer.

RELATIONSHIPS BREAKDOWN

When decisions are made to go into a relationship, the main focus is to make it a right environment. Create the appropriate atmosphere to live in harmony for self and others. When this ideal goes pear shaped, the damage can be heart rending. To literally sit down to articulate what you are going through with others can be difficult, as sometimes those who posed as helpers are also responsible for igniting the problem: "O Lord, truly I am your servant; I am your servant, the son of your maidservant: You have freed me from my chains."

Psalm 116:16 NIV

Problems are the major cause of disruption. When breakdown occurs it is like a form of chain, which binds individuals.

The chains of lovers are wonderful when things are at their best but when it is sour, then deliverance should be sought. To eat your food in sorrow, sleep in fear and despair, move around as if on tenterhooks, disassociate from others who could profit you, lose your peace of mind and self worth, seeing everything as dismal and gloomy. If this is how you are left feeling, then it is time to seek the Lord that this chain be broken. Life without fun, laughter, joy, appreciation, being respected and being valued is meaningless and almost a waste of space, time and energy, if equilibrium is not entwined.

Here is a list of possible chains that bind when things go wrong. They are:

Loss of home

Loss of fellowship

Loss of finance

Loss of status

Loss of children

Loss of self worth

Loss of health

Loss of peace of mind

Loss of focus

The veil of cover up is visibly exposed before God and He
cannot be tricked to believe a lie.
Therefore to give way so that the problem cripples you is
just not an option! Even when the dread of lifelessness
surrounds you, keep hope alive and forge ahead.
Focus on things above. The Lord is for all those whose
trust is in Him.
There is no gain without pain. We lose to win. We engage
in combat to acquire the victory.

Shall the failure of the past be the master of your future?

The breakdown of that relationship should not be to your
detriment but to your advancement.
Satan knows how much this is hurting you and it is one of
his strategic tools to hold you ransom. God has given you
the power to break Satan's stronghold and for you to escape
the snares of the fowler.

Things will only go un-noticed for a little while and then the truth will be revealed. Make sure though that you are in the clear. If not, be quick to repent because the Lord God is just in His dealings with all human beings.

Tamar's family predicament could only last for as long as she was unprepared to tackle it. Once she rose up, Satan's work and days were numbered. Heaven stood with her and God empowered her to win triumphantly.
The said legacy of God's help and blessing is reserved for you to access and make good use of.

FINDING YOUR NICHE

Fate would have it that many people only find their rightful place and position after a dramatic participation in a life changing experience. What we go through either makes us better or worse.

For the greater part, many will vouch that it made them look at life differently. They have become wiser through it, because through it, they can be considered as positive role models. They can shed light on what to do when faced with dark paths or trouble of a similar nature. It is at these times that the invisible hand of God is at work and our guardian angel steps in and aids us on the journey.

When you are feeling totally incapable, incompetent and fragile in managing your problems, it is then that you have the chance to come face to face with who you really are. The decision has to be made and it has to be here and now. The day Tamar decided to play the role of a prostitute in order to prove her adversaries wrong was the said day she turned her life around, just as in Hagar's case:

" Your servant is in your hands, Abram said. Do with her whatever you think best. Then Sarai ill-treated Hagar; So she fled from her. The angel of the Lord found Hagar near a spring in the desert; It was the spring that is beside the road to Shur. And he said, Hagar, servant of Sarai, where have you come from, and where are you going? I'm running away from my mistress Sarai, she answered. Then the angel of the Lord told her, go back to your mistress and submit to her. The angel added, I will so increase your descendants that they will be too numerous to count."

Genesis 16:6-10 NIV.

Hagar's bad treatment by Sarai, her mistress, caused her to leave home, taking nothing but her pregnant self, for the sake of peace of mind.

It was during this period that she experienced the visitation of Christ, through the means of the angels. She was friendless, homeless, and penniless.

God gave her a revelation that motivated her to live on, to return home and to look to a bright future.

This is not just for Hagar, but also for everyone who is called and is committed to the Will of God.

STAYING AT THE TOP

It is the Lord's responsibility to sustain us and to secure us from falling. The beauty of God driven promotion is that it lasts as long as we are prepared to remain faithful to His Lordship and Shepherding care.

The Lord's promotion is not like the world's idea of how promotion is to be. Our experience of ideal promotion is a fragile one, and for the greater part it is as long as you comply with the expectation outlined for the job or the position.

Our criteria can be so very different to the Lord's. Look at the list and see if you can identify with any aspect of it:

If your face fits – Then you are in.

If your personality blends in – Then you are a part.

If you have the right qualifications and experience – Then you stand a chance to become a part of that company or group.

If your colour is right – then you are in.

If your accent is right – Then you will be considered suitable.

The Lord's criteria are very different.

If your heart is right – Then God is with you to help you.

If you seek God's guidance – Then you will be prosperous.

If you lack wisdom, knowledge and understanding – Then the Lord will give you bountifully.

If you are in trouble and call to the Lord – then He promises to hear you and help you.

The Lord's choice is eternally validated. It states: "But God chose the foolish things of the world to shame the wise; God chose the weak things of the world to shame the strong. He chose the lowly things of this world and the despised things and the things that are not to nullify the things that are, so that no one may boast before Him."

1 Corinthians 1:26–29 NIV.

Whoever the Lord promotes no man can demote. The Lord does not require any of us to have already attained and possess innate extreme qualities, because He has at His disposal, every power and authority to call things into being for us His chosen children. The word of the Lord states: "If any of you lacks wisdom, he should ask God, who gives generously to all without finding fault, and it will be given to him." James 1: 5 NIV

Genuineness is not on the surface for everyone to behold, like diamond it is difficult to come by. So only the diligent in mind and spirit will function as 'a cut above the rest'.

It is therefore our responsibility to take note and the necessary action required, to change our personal ways. It is needful then to curb our sinful nature, so that the Lord will be pleased to keep us at the top in a famous position.

If staying in the same circle is not doing it for you then move into a new one.

Tamar rose to the top never to be subjected to the dark path she was once constrained to. You and I must face our enemies and maintain our stand in getting and staying at the top, with the Divine help of God on our side.

CHANGE FOR GENERATIONS TO COME

The era that God has brought us in is an exiting one. It is technologically charged, with much challenge ahead of us. To become proactive at such a time like this is to sacrificially bring self under control and move into the arena of change.

Our God specialises in doing new things. It is my view that God gets bored with the same old same old. Therefore, make every effort to release yourself from that dreaded oppressive trap, and witness the magic of God's wonder taking place in you and for you. He said: "See, the former things have taken place, and new things I declare; before they spring into being I announce them to you."

Isaiah 42:9 NIV

The awesome God of heaven is standing for our attention to bring to pass our request. I believe Tamar prayed, fasted, wished and hoped for change but it was far from her, until she decided enough was enough. She bravely closed the doors of barrenness, non-progress and complacency and forced open the door of opportunity.

Are there some doors that you need to make a firm decision on closing? So when will this be?

Is there a right time and a wrong time?

In the calendar of our agenda, it is easy to dither and to find ourselves negating our chances to move on whilst the time swiftly passes us by, but the Lord implores us to redeem the time.

One seemingly insignificant action of Tamar, rippled into a vast wealth of God's blessings upon her life and generations to come. The 'what's' and 'ifs' did not get an occasion to rule but instead were obliterated from Tamar's destiny.

Tamar brought lasting change to her world such as:

The sound of babies crying

The sound of laughter from children

The sound of playing in and outside of the home

Two outstanding nations, Perez and Zerah

Restoration of her self-importance

Becoming a proud and honoured ancestor

Tamar became a beacon for all to emulate in the generation of Judah and Israel as a nation!

The word of the Lord has a magic formula enshrined in it that guarantees prosperity and victory. It states: "I took you from the ends of the earth, from its farthest corners I called you. I said, 'You are my servant'; I have chosen you and have not rejected you. So do not fear, for I am with you; do not be dismayed, for I am your God. I will strengthen you and help you; I will uphold you with my righteous right hand."

Isaiah 41:9-10 NIV

Fear is the enemy's strongest strategy to hold people bound. With a renewed mind, however, and determination of heart, nothing can stand in the way of change. No devils, no powers, no principalities, no wicked person or system, because the Lord gives power, boldness, wisdom, knowledge and understanding for each situation.

Those whose confidence is in the Lord can bask in the assurance that their change is for the better, though painful this may feel. Don't ever forget that at the time of childbirth it is one of the most painful periods in a woman's life but it is all natural, according to God's purpose. Just as this type of pain is not permanent, neither are our problems and heartache, if we will entreat the Lord to advocate and Shepherd us.

Assurances from the word of the Lord are as follows:
"The God of peace will soon crush Satan under your feet.
The grace of our Lord Jesus be with you."
Romans 16:20 NIV

"Be joyful always; pray continually; give thanks in all circumstances, for this is God's will for you in Christ Jesus. Do not put out the Spirit's fire; do not treat prophecies with contempt. Test everything. Hold on to the good. Avoid every kind of evil. May God Himself, the God of peace, sanctify you through and through! May your whole spirit, soul and body be kept blameless at the coming of our Lord

Jesus Christ. The one who calls you is faithful and He will do it."

1 Thessalonians 5:16-24 NIV

With the favour of God Tamar changed. Countless other women have changed. Dorothy has changed; thus it is your time to get up and take action to change for yourself and generations to come.

Change now, before change overtakes you and changes you into what you don't want. The power is invested in you to be positively promoted.

SELF HEALING EXERCISES – 8

Brave your problems to change them.

When problems come they arrive with a large company, all of which comes to mould, shape or break you!

Consider making a list of positives and negatives of your journey so far, this will help you to see the wood from the trees.

When you have done so, the problems are no longer trapped within you but they are now outside of you.

If indeed they are now external then you have excelled to become the manager of that situation.

Own the positives

Deal with the negatives

And grow from both!

Jesus wants to heal you, look closely at the scriptures: "Jesus went through Galilee, teaching in their synagogues, preaching the good news of the Kingdom, and healing every disease and sickness among the people"
St. Matthew 4: 23 NIV

In like manner the word of the Lord is constantly encouraging us to draw near to God for every healing, it said: "How God anointed Jesus of Nazareth with the Holy Spirit and power and how He went around doing good and healing all who were under the power of the devil, because God was with Him."
Acts 10: 38 NIV

Don't walk away from your healing; take it. It's yours! Jesus alone paid the price for your release from all that attempted to destroy you.

PRAYER - 9

WHO NEEDS TO PRAY?

Prayer is one of our greatest weapons and if you don't know how to use it for your benefit, you will suffer when the battles of life wages war against you. Everyone needs to pray constantly, regardless of position, because life is uncertain, fragile and volatile.

To overcome many difficulties, the art of praying to a source bigger than ones reliance in the universe is essential.

I personally found that God the Sovereign One, who governs all things, gives close attention to the prayers made directly to Him, out of a genuine heart.

You do not need any fancy words, or a particular order or style; just be yourself, saying what you are experiencing in the way that you best express yourself, at any time, anywhere.

There are great blessings to be gained from talking to the Lord, He won't tell anyone else, because God is more than confidential!

He won't assume what you might be experiencing because He is in it with you.

He won't make you feel foolish or ignore your plea for help.

He will give you instant peace and reassurance that He is with you and will be with you.

The prayer of David said: "Give ear to my words, O Lord, consider my sighing. Listen to my cry for help, my King and my God, for to you I pray." Psalm 5:1-2 NIV

Humans are tripartite beings.

Body – Deals with the five senses: Smelling, hearing, tasting, feeling and seeing

Soul - Deals with the intellect: Reasoning, decision-making, judgement etc.

Spirit – Deals with connecting us with God our creator, the higher realm beyond the physical.

Our spirit never sleeps; as long as we are within this earthly body it is active even when we are asleep or unconscious.

Having then the discipline to bring all three parts together, body, soul and spirit, under the shepherding care of the Lord, is rewarding for the individual, who will call upon the Lord and trust His word.

Ephesians 6:12 NIV states: "For our struggle is not against flesh and blood, but against the rulers, against the authorities, against the powers of this dark world and against the spiritual forces of evil in the heavenly realms."

Communicating our feelings, pains and experiences in prayer to the Lord is the surest way forward.

If possible find someone, you can trust and pray candidly with, but if you can't, it does not matter. James 5:16 NIV said: "Therefore confess your sins to each other and pray for each other so that you may be healed. The prayer of a righteous man (woman) is powerful and effective."

FASTING - 10

This means going without food for the time you have determined.

During the time of fasting there are great benefits to be derived for the betterment of your good plans before Almighty God.

There are groups of people in our world who fast to fulfil wicked schemes and they get their desires.

How much more is it then, for those who will make the Lord the pivotal focus of their heart's ambition in times of fasting for change? The Lord said: "Is not this the kind of fasting I have chosen: To loose the chains of injustice and untie the cords of the yoke, to set the oppressed free and break every yoke?"
Isaiah 58:6 NIV

Make prayer your food during the time you have set aside to fast!

How to fast is dependant on your circumstances before you begin the fast; your health, your emotions, your mindset etc. Start slowly if you have never done so before. Begin with half a day, progress to a full day and build up a resistance to having the usual food intake. Try going for days according to your ability.

It is advisable to drink clear fluid to avoid dehydration. Those of you who are on medication should seek the advice of your Doctor before you begin.

The purpose of fasting is to improve your health and well-being, not decrease it. The Spirit of the Lord will aid you if you consult with the Lord before your start.

THE PHYSICIAN - 11

In our Western world most people have an attachment with a physician known as General Practitioner (GP). When those who are registered with them are not feeling well, from adults to children, they are the first point of call.

Many people are in constant reliance on their Doctor for daily advice, medicine, and guidance, just like a woman Jesus assisted: "And a woman was there who had been subject to bleeding for twelve years. She had suffered a great deal under the care of many Doctors and had spent all she had; yet instead of getting better she grew worse. When she heard about Jesus, she came up behind Him in the crowd and touched His cloak, because she thought, "If I just touch His clothes, I will be healed." Immediately her bleeding stopped and she felt in her body that she was freed from her suffering."

St. Mark 5:25-29 NIV

The Most Holy God of heaven and earth, through His precious Son Jesus Christ, is our powerful physician. He has never diagnosed a case incorrectly, He succeeds where others fail, and He brings the impossibilities into existence, for the sake of His own name and for our good.

Your condition is not out of God's reach; the Lord is Supreme and Awesome in His wonder to bring you healing, deliverance and permanent change! So whether you are experiencing:

Physical

Spiritual

Emotional

Sexual

Financial

Social

Or any other condition, the bottom line is, Jesus is our unfailing physician, but we must exercise our faith to receive His impartial and true healing.

Many people trust only the physician who they can see and doubt the existence of the invisible God and His power to help when they are in dire illness. Here is a very good example: "In the thirty ninth year of his reign Asa was afflicted with a disease in his feet. Though his disease was

severe, even in his illness he did not seek help from the
Lord, but only from the physicians."
2 Chronicles 16:12 NIV

What do you think may have happened in Asa's illness,
concerning his relationship with the Lord? Many people
feel frustrated and perplexed when they are directly affected
as fear and doubt is rife during these moments. Hence it is
essential that we do not forget the Lord as Asa clearly or
stubbornly did. Asa knew of God's grace and mercy yet he
did not call upon the Lord, when he needed to do so.

How do you view God right now in your situation?

The ability is invested in you to change your mind
concerning the Lord and His concern for you!

The Lord Jesus is our true physician; all knowledge, power,
wisdom and every disease are under His domain to control
and heal.
Is there anything too hard for God?

ATTACHMENT AND FELLOWSHIP - 12

The whole rationale for having friendship is to share in comparable ideals, and to grow together in peace and harmony. When this ideal is distorted, be it in the:

Immediate family unit

The extended family

The group that attachment is formed

The work colleagues

The community that you belongs to, etc.
Then it is time to rethink the exact benefit it has for you personally.

Any attachment must help to bring wholeness to your life. If you have outgrown or have become a misfit, consider embracing change. Don't ever, do nothing! Positive rapport is yours to have and to be apart of! As the word of the Lord states:

"God who has called you into fellowship with His Son Jesus Christ our Lord, is faithful." 1 Corinthians 1:8 NIV

Unfaithfulness is rampant in our time but God is faithful.

The Lord will never detach Himself from any of us, irrespective of how challenging we are. How reassuring! Jesus' attachment to us is forever and eternally fixed, if we abide in Him and His word abides in us.

SELF ESTEEM - 13

To think less of your self than you ought to is a crime.

When the world thinks the worst of you, try not to subject your mind to the same thinking. You have been fearfully and wonderfully made: you are not ordinary even though you are feeling terrible right now. This is temporary.

Being put down must become a thing of the past.

Being subjected to harsh criticism must come to an abrupt end.

Looking downward, wishing your life away must end with your determination by entreating the Lord's favour.

As it is written: "By myself I can do nothing; I judge only as I hear, and my judgement is just, for I seek not to please myself but Him who sent me." St John 5: 30 NIV

Raise your faith, raise your expectation and ultimately you will raise your self-esteem.

High self esteem comes readily when things are going as planned, but when life's storms blow and push you out of your depth, then not only does low self esteem set in, but the company of poor self esteem also comes along to cast upon you a long sentence in the hope of constraining and restraining you.

Many therapists are at hand to walk you through the rough path of low and poor self-esteem, but there is none as powerful as the Lord and His Holy word to lift you permanently. You cannot compete with a Christian therapist as they draw virtues from the Lord and in turn invest this into you.

ACCEPT CHANGE TO MOVE ON - **14**

Change takes us out of our comfort zones. It is quite a difficult thing to embrace, therefore to accept change when you haven't planned for it can be a daunting experience. Nevertheless, it is a journey for only one at a time, and fortunately you are chosen as the head of this change:

Whether it is a:

Change of job

Change of home

Change of family circle

Change of leadership

Change of friends

Change of country

Change of status

Change of fellowship

Change of name

Change of mindset

Change of attitude

Or Change of the familiar

Whatever you do, don't be caught not being flexible to accept your moment to grow because of the change before you!

The Lord alone is unchanging: "I the Lord do not change. So you, O descendants of Jacob, are not destroyed."

Malachi 3:6 NIV

SET TARGETS - 15

It is extremely important to start again by setting personal targets, even though you may be feeling worn out and tired by the forgone experiences.

It is very possible to have your latter life better than the former.

When life hits you with an indelible blow with a wicked plan to destroy your destiny, then the courage to fight back is your only hope and guess what? God is in the fight with you to win back all you have lost!

You can then celebrate God's grace, goodness, mercy, loving-kindness and Sovereignty over all life's problems.

The Lord will guide you and help you to:

Laugh again – Immeasurable Joy

Sing again – Music to the soul

Love again – Fulfilment of all human needs

Trust again – Key to being in charge

Strong again – Having the resilience to conquer

God will undoubtedly give you back all and more that was taken away from you, as He had done with so many others before you.

He is the only one in and above the universe that has the power to bring lasting change to you and your future generations, as He did for Tamar and her sons.

Who are you? What are you? You are special!
Psalm 37:5 NIV said: "Commit your way to the Lord; trust in Him and He will do this."

WHAT ELSE - 16

For those of you who would like to know what else is in store, please read on.

Tamar is a Ministry that holds regular conferences, entitled Tamar Ministry 'Healing Hurting Women'. It is an interdenominational gathering of God's people. Also there are intensive workshops training sessions taking place in England which cover:

❖ Personal empowerment and mentoring

❖ Empowering and equipping women to fulfil the aims and objectives of Tamar Ministry

❖ Women in need of healing and or personal counselling

If your desire beyond the reading of this book is to be a part of this Ministry or to see Tamar Ministry happening in your area then do not hesitate to make the necessary contact, via email or write to: d.guy37@ntlworld.com

Tamar Ministry Healing Hurting Women

PO BOX 7113, Chellaston, Derby, DE1 0BL, UK

SCRIPTURE REFERENCES - 17

PAGES	QUOTES/	SCRIPTURES
P.9	Who alone does wondrous	Psalm 72:18
P.12	Bless me indeed, enlarge	1 Chronicles 4:10
P.16	Set lonely in family	Psalm 68:6
P.19	Spirit intercedes	Romans 8:26-27
P.21	Then the Lord God made a woman	Genesis 2:22
P.27	Judge not less ye be judged	Matthew 7:1-2
P.31	Two prostitutes and a live baby	1 King 3:26-28
P.32	Bitterly she weeps at night	Lamentations 1:2
P.34	His eyes are on the ways of men	Job 34:21-22
P.35	Eyes of the Lord are everywhere	Proverbs 15:3
P.36	Wicked in the Lord's sight	Genesis 38:7
P.39	Lie with your brother's wife	Genesis 38:8
P.41	Above repeated	Genesis 38:8
P.42	Take heed you senseless ones	Psalm 94:8-9
P.43	Spilled his semen on the ground	Genesis 38:9-10
P.44	The heavens praise your wonders	Psalm 89:5-8
P.47	Spirit of the Lord is on me	Isaiah 61:1-3
P.48	The word of a gossip	Proverbs 18:8
P.49	Fear not I have redeemed	Isaiah 43:1-3
P.51	There is no wisdom	Proverbs 21:30
P.53	Now the serpent was more	Genesis 3:1

en.wikipedia.org/wiki/Levirate_marriage